THE SUNDAY TIMES

Develop Your PR Skills

Neil Richardson and Lucy Laville

KoganPage

LONDON PHILADELPHIA NEW DELHI

Publisher's note

Every possible effort has been made to ensure that the information contained in this book is accurate at the time of going to press, and the publishers and authors cannot accept responsibility for any errors or omissions, however caused. No responsibility for loss or damage occasioned to any person acting, or refraining from action, as a result of the material in this publication can be accepted by the editor, the publisher or either of the authors.

First published in Great Britain and the United States in 2010 by Kogan Page Limited

120 Pentonville Road	525 South 4th Street, #241	4737/23 Ansari Road
London N1 9JN	Philadelphia PA 19147	Daryaganj
United Kingdom	USA	New Delhi 110002
www.koganpage.com		India

© Neil Richardson and Lucy Laville, 2010

The right of Neil Richardson and Lucy Laville to be identified as the authors of this work has been asserted by them in accordance with the Copyright, Designs and Patents Act 1988.

ISBN   978 0 7494 5970 3
E-ISBN   978 0 7494 5971 0

The views expressed in this book are those of the authors, and are not necessarily the same as those of Times Newspapers Ltd.

British Library Cataloguing-in-Publication Data

A CIP record for this book is available from the British Library.

Library of Congress Cataloging-in-Publication Data

Richardson, Neil.
    Develop your PR skills / Lucy Laville, Neil Richardson.
        p. cm.
    Includes bibliographical references.
    ISBN 978-0-7494-5970-3 -- ISBN 978-0-7494-5971-0 (ebook) 1. Public relations.
I. Laville, Lucy. II. Title.
    HD59.R47 2010
    659.2--dc22
                    2010000342

Typeset by Saxon Graphics Ltd, Derby
Printed and bound in India by Replika Press Pvt Ltd

Contents

Introduction

First, thank you for buying this book. Having bought it, you are now one of our customers, which means a lot to us. Throughout the text you'll see the theme of public relations (PR) being a major driver of stakeholder satisfaction and competitive advantage. These are arguably the most important factors for many professionals.

If you're not a PR practitioner, you may wonder whether it really matters. Suffice it to say that substantial research has proved the need for good-quality PR for most companies. As Senior Lecturers at Leeds Business School, we have considerable experience of teaching across the whole range of ages, industrial experiences, organisational types and markets. In teaching professional students (working towards Chartered status) we are often asked a diverse range of questions. We've encapsulated these questions in this text and offered honest, sometimes critical, answers. The professional students, studying in their spare time, are truly representative of the whole spectrum of organisations and businesses.

PR can benefit all organisations, whether public, private or third sector. It can help you identify, build and maintain relationships with your publics, including customers and prospects, as well as wider groups of individuals who may influence your organisation. Understanding these groups and how to communicate with them effectively is crucial in maintaining and developing your organisation's reputation.

This book is designed to provide those with little or no understanding of PR with a practical guide on how to use it to enhance and develop your business opportunities. So whether you work for a small company, multinational, charity or sole trader, or if you simply want to explore the opportunities of a career in PR, this book will provide you with the foundations to understanding how PR can help you build your success.

This text is aimed at practitioners who do not have the time to trawl through 1,200-page tomes. That said, our approach, using examples to apply PR theories, will offer insights into the theories missing from many key texts. We're confident you will find new information that will enable you to develop your knowledge, skills and, hopefully, attitude.

Throughout the text we've suggested activities designed to encourage you to re-evaluate your surroundings. Questions are posed throughout with answers at the back (not that you'd cheat). There has to be a test! Despite having decades of private-sector experience between us, we're academics, after all!

So once again, thanks for the order and enjoy the book.

1

Public relations in business: an introduction

Many people consider PR to be all about media relations: how to get your name in newspapers and trade magazines, or on radio or TV, whether at a local, regional or national level. Many PR practitioners do indeed spend a lot of their time developing press opportunities and they now have the added challenge and huge opportunities offered by internet communications via social networking sites and blogs as well as websites.

We explore these areas of media and new media relations in more detail in later chapters. It is, however, important to understand that PR is much more than media relations; it can be highly effective in helping you to manage relationships with staff, suppliers, members, community groups, investors, influencers, and new and existing customers as well as in dealing with crises and issues in an ever-changing world.

What is PR?

In its simplest form, public relations is about developing and managing relations with stakeholders. Taking a strategic approach to public relations will ensure that the tactics you implement, from sending press releases to the media to communicating with staff, investors and other audiences, are most effective and sustainable.

The profession

PR's roots in business can be traced back to the 19th century, when the showman, entrepreneur and 'icon of American spirit' PT Barnum famously said, 'Without promotion something terrible happens, nothing!' In the early 1900s, Edward Bernays, a nephew of Sigmund Freud, was a publicist for the arts who wrote books about the power of persuasion and techniques for success that are still influential today.

Public relations is a relatively new profession, although fundamentally it is about engaging communication tactics to influence the public, which has been done by governments, dictators and key influencers for hundreds of years. The growing profession is represented in the United Kingdom by the Chartered Institute of Public Relations (CIPR), a professional body that was established in 1948 and awarded chartered status in 2005. PR is used in a vast range of industries and professions, with different skills and competences being employed by practitioners. It is still emerging as a discipline and is therefore difficult to define in a simple way.

Despite its relatively new arrival as a recognised discipline, it has become one of the most popular professions for graduates, and a range of professional and academic qualifications have been developed over the past decade.

Industry definition

The UK's CIPR defines PR as:

being about reputation – the result of what you do, what you say and what others say about you... Public relations is the discipline which looks after reputation, with the aim of earning understanding and support and influencing opinion and behaviour. It is the planned and sustained effort to establish and maintain goodwill and mutual understanding between an organisation and its publics.

In essence this definition, if used in its truest form, is about PR becoming so embedded in an organisation's culture and vision that it permeates through all aspects of the organisation. Whether it needs a dedicated PR practitioner to implement this is debatable, but it does require the desire of the managing director or CEO and top management to embed this culture within the organisation, whatever its size and the complexity of its business.

The people involved

PR practitioners, at a tactical level, are often called 'PRs', press officers, media relations managers or communications officers. At a strategic level, PRs may be called PR managers, heads of PR or communications directors. A recent survey of FTSE 100 companies revealed that, while all have a PR/communications department, most have a PR/communications specialist at board level, contributing to strategic decisions about the direction of the organisation.

Investment at board level is obviously expensive but demonstrates how important big businesses view PR as being – as a discipline that adds value to their organisation. Similarly, public-sector organisations, including (in the United Kingdom) the National Health Service, councils and government departments, invest heavily in PR campaigns and activities to build and maintain relations with their publics.

What PR is not

PR is not marketing, advertising, sponsorship, sales or any of the more obvious expensive tools that send a message directly to 'customers', often saying, 'We are great, buy our products.' PR is more subtle: 'You may have heard about us; get to know us and we may have a long and happy relationship.' PR does not need to involve the big costs that advertising and sponsorship incur, and while it is often used to complement these tactics, it can be just as effective as a stand-alone discipline.

Propaganda and spin

The PR industry has been associated with propaganda, no more so than during times of war or when used by dictators, when the messages communicated are based on ideals rather than reality. Criticism is often aimed at businesses and organisations that do not 'practise what they preach', or spin the story to include a heavily biased opinion in favour of the message sender. Spin doctors – PR practitioners representing political parties – are frequently criticised for their part in manipulating the truth or being economical with the truth.

In the United Kingdom there are certain laws to protect individuals who are exploited by these means. Cases of libel action being brought against PR practitioners are rare, but high-profile practitioners such as Max Clifford, who would regard himself as a publicist rather than a PR practitioner, have found themselves facing High Court rulings for promoting stories that were falsified. Similarly, newspapers are treated with the same legal action for reporting stories, often promoted by PRs, that are defamatory and may cause huge anxiety for those misrepresented.

Despite this reputation, the result of activities practised by a small minority, there is much valuable work done by PR practitioners who represent charities, businesses, political parties and public-sector organisations as well as individuals. The chartered status of the profession and the public debates around morality and mutual benefit have led to a valued profession with growing respect as a creative and strategic industry. The relationship between PRs and journalists is increasingly based on mutual respect, with much fluidity between the professions. People with a background in journalism make up a large number of PRs as they look to diversify and develop as communicators. Salaries and working conditions are often more favourable in the PR industry than for most journalists working in a media industry that is in decline as more of us turn to the internet to get our news.

Credibility and trust are paramount in good PR. Communicated messages based on fact and the credibility of the message sender are crucial to effective PR. The audience, whether they are reading about you in a newspaper or on the internet, or are hearing you speak at an event or conference, must believe you have the authority, based on truths and trust, to engage in a mutually beneficial relationship. As the communicator, you must recognise that gaining this trust is important to building mutually beneficial relationships with your audiences that will sustain positive outcomes for your organisation.

Strategy or tactics?

Mutual respect is the most effective way to develop your reputation and build long and fruitful relationships with your stakeholders, whether they are customers, staff, investors, suppliers, community groups or even activist groups that may oppose the activities of your business. This is crucial to developing an understanding of the value that PR can add to your organisation. Identifying your target publics, the effect they have on your organisation and how to develop a mutually beneficial relationship with them is crucial to implementing effective PR.

Planning a sustained programme of PR activities that has clear aims and objectives, and evaluating the results, will ensure that you maximise the PR potentials for your organisation. A PR strategy might involve a six-month campaign focusing on one specific element of your business or a broader and longer campaign that involves a company-wide strategy. Whatever your PR strategy is aiming to achieve, it can be supported with a range of individual programmes of PR activity and tactics being implemented. Chapter 3 explores in more detail how to plan a strategic campaign and provides a framework for developing your own PR strategy, which includes setting objectives, developing tactics and evaluating outputs and outcomes.

Many companies will use regular PR tactics such as media releases, corporate literature, events, in-house magazines, or attending industry conferences without fully understanding the impact of these individual strands of activity, never mind the collective impact of using a range of tactics. We all know that it is important to maintain communication with audiences via a range of activities, but understanding the aim of these individual and collective activities will ensure that the most successful ones are used to their maximum benefit and that any ineffective activities are improved upon or not deployed in the future.

Whilst many consider PR to be a relatively cheap alternative to other communication tools such as advertising, sponsorship and many marketing activities, it still requires a big investment in time and resources, and must be taken seriously and with great consideration as to its ongoing effects and outcomes.

Legal boundaries

In an increasingly litigious world there are legal frameworks that regulate business and ensure that it operates legally, ethically and fairly. A number of Acts of the UK Parliament have certainly provided a framework for PR practitioners within which to operate both legally and ethically. The Libel Act 1792, the Data Protection Act 1998, the Freedom of Information Act 2000 and the Privacy Law 1987 are crucial to protect the activities of many practitioners as well as act as a boundary for ethical practice.

The EU Directive on Information and Consultation of Employees (2004) gives employees of 'undertakings of 50 or more employees' rights to be informed and consulted about issues that affect their employment and the prospect of the business. This, in turn, has led to the need for employers to communicate more effectively with staff via internal communication strategies that are increasingly designed and delivered by PR practitioners rather than human resources (HR) departments.

Practical considerations

The following chapters will give you the tools to be more proactive and effective in managing PR activities and will show you how to use it, from getting the most out of employees through to encouraging journalists to say good things about your business.

Many small to medium-sized enterprises (SMEs) outsource their PR activities, or alternatively it may be the sole or part of the responsibility of a single individual. Often these activities will be monitored or actioned by managers who see PR as an important part of business development and critical to the success of the organisation. Larger organisations may well have several PR practitioners employed by the business as well as using the services of PR agencies, especially for specific campaigns that require specialist knowledge that PR agencies can provide. Many PR agencies specialise in sectors or disciplines because, for example, they have strong contacts in the trade publications, understand legislation, have relevant government or financial expertise or have experience of key stakeholder relations.

If you want to explore developing a PR role within your organisation, you can gather information about practitioner responsibilities by studying the jobs pages of *PR Week* and the Media supplement of *The Guardian*. Both have websites with job adverts and a list of specifications for practitioners as well as salary guides. Chapter 10 explores in more detail the cost implications of using PR practitioners, from recruiting staff to using PR agencies and consultancies.

Hiring a PR agency

There is a wide spectrum of professional support available to you via agencies. If you're unsure about which communications tools to use (and assuming you can afford the fees), it may be wise to use an agency. But which sort? The United Kingdom has some of the world's most innovative and successful PR agencies. They include the large, full-service agencies such as Saatchi & Saatchi, which can create, develop, plan and execute any manner of communication campaign as they employ specialists in all aspects of communication and have vast resources. Hence, such organisations can service the whole of the marketing communications (marcomms) mix (see Figure 2.1, page 14) on your behalf.

Alternatively, you could use an independent specialist PR agency. This choice would be generally cheaper as smaller companies do not have vast overheads to service. However, while they could create fantastic PR for you, you might still need additional types of communication, such as a sales promotion. The benefit of using a full-service agency is that it will house all marcomms specialists under one roof and can therefore cross-coordinate all communication activities on your behalf. However, it comes at a cost.

If you are thinking of hiring a PR agency or consultant, you may find the following useful:

- *A good degree of fit.* Different PR agencies specialise in different areas. Some are better at promoting established businesses, whereas others are more focused on newly formed companies. The PR agency should have local, regional and national press contacts; its previous work should illustrate whether that is the case.
- *Company and sector knowledge.* It is imperative that the agency understands what your company does – its culture, its marketplace and what makes it special or unique. Be cautious if the people you talk to do not appear interested in taking the time to understand your company.
- *Track record.* It's a cliché, but 'a good PR agency is a busy PR agency', so ask for copies of press releases and media coverage that the agency has generated for clients in the past. Ask for testimonials from clients. You need to benchmark them, as agencies charge differing amounts

for various tasks. Issues such as typical rates are addressed in Chapter 10. However, rates alone will not tell you the full story. The key to establishing a reasonable PR budget is to determine what agencies charge for a range of services and how many hours of creative time it takes to complete these projects.

Summary and activities

Key points

- PR provides benefits for *all* organisations – big or small, public, private or not-for-profit. SMEs particularly are often unaware of the benefits of good PR.
- There is more to PR than simply media relations.
- Before you decide which communication tools to use to deliver your message from sender to receiver, there are a number of factors to consider that will help you choose the most appropriate communication tools and, indeed, the configuration of the message you send.

Questions

1. At which levels of business does PR operate?
2. How do legal constraints impact on PR?
3. Who can undertake PR responsibilities?

Activities

The following represent UK- and European-based PR websites that host a wealth of information:

- The Chartered Institute of Public Relations' website, http://www.cipr.co.uk, has useful sections such as

'Looking for PR,' which includes definitions, a glossary and a guide to hiring a PR consultant, plus a PR directory.

- MediaUK (website: http://www.mediauk.com) is a forum for discussion and information for UK PR professionals plus an excellent UK media internet directory and a listing of the latest media news.

- The European Public Relations Confederation (website: http://www.cerp.org) is the umbrella organisation of national and professional PR associations all over Europe.

- The Science, Technology, Engineering and Medicine Public Relations Association (website: http://www. stempra.org.uk).

2

Where PR sits with advertising and marketing

Over the years, companies' marketing communications (or comms) activities have increased in importance, becoming a key factor in our lives. Whether we create and send messages to the marketplace or receive (and react) to them, it's fair to say that 'comms' activities are part and parcel of our daily routines. A criticism aimed at marketing in general is that there are so many products and services competing for our attention that we're subjected to a barrage of chatter or 'noise'. This wall of noise is regarded by some as being all-pervasive and as interfering with how you conduct basic comms with your customers and prospects.

There are a variety of different comms techniques and tools (Figure 2.1), and they can be used to achieve a large number of differing objectives. The diagram is not exhaustive and the list of objectives is changing every day – often driven by new technological developments.

Many language theorists argue that written words are more powerful than spoken words. However, most marketers (academics and practitioners alike) believe that 'word of mouth' is the most powerful means of communication. This has now morphed into 'word of mouse' in the domain of blogs, social

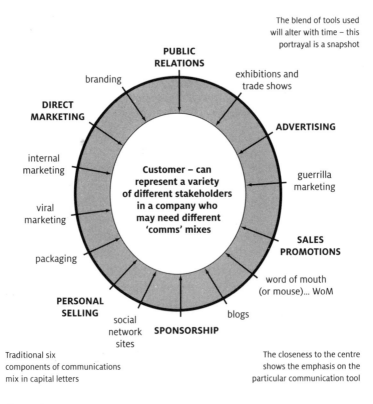

The blend of tools used will alter with time – this portrayal is a snapshot

PUBLIC RELATIONS

branding

exhibitions and trade shows

DIRECT MARKETING

ADVERTISING

internal marketing

guerrilla marketing

viral marketing

Customer – can represent a variety of different stakeholders in a company who may need different 'comms' mixes

packaging

SALES PROMOTIONS

word of mouth (or mouse)... WoM

PERSONAL SELLING

social network sites

blogs

SPONSORSHIP

Traditional six components of communications mix in capital letters

The closeness to the centre shows the emphasis on the particular communication tool

Figure 2.1 Expanded comms mix

network sites, public forums and comparison websites. In 2009, Twitter became the marketing channel of the chattering classes. Followers could read the tweets of supposed style leaders. Numerous celebrities then employed skilled communicators to tweet on their behalf – which seems to defeat the point. Hence, if you intend using such tools you'll need to develop an aptitude for understanding which tool, or combination of tools, will allow you to achieve your objectives.

Some authors use the term 'promotional mix', but this can be confusing as some customers (or prospects) may believe you're referring to 'sales promotions' rather than 'communication'. If you keep terms clean and simple, less confusion will result. Also, promotion implies a monologue whereas 'comms' suggests a dialogue, which is healthier and in the long term more profitable.

PR and advertising

Let us consider the chapter title as a series of questions. That is, where does PR sit, say, with advertising? You'd think that this question would be simple to answer. However, as with most things in life, understanding how marketing works is more complex than most people initially believe.

When you watch advertisements on TV, it's often easier to remember the gimmick (eg the drumming gorilla) than the central message (eg the chocolate). Cunning puns and use of synonyms can avoid this (eg 'compare the meerkat' versus 'compare the market'), but often the message is lost. If you doubt this, try a quick exercise. Write down in the next 10 seconds the advert you saw yesterday that made the biggest impression on you. It doesn't have to be a favourable impression – just the one that really sticks in your memory. What was the brand? What was the central message the advertiser was trying to communicate? Now write down the adverts that preceded and followed your initial choice... Struggling? Join the club! It's an exercise that most people tend to struggle with. Why can't you remember a few ads and their central messages? This is a by-product of noise.

Hence, you need to develop (or buy in) the skills used by good communicators in order to realistically appreciate challenges presented by the aforementioned noise. You need to create comms that penetrate the all-pervading clutter so that your message is the key piece of communication your customers and prospects actually identify with, recall and respond to.

Some think PR stands apart from marketing, and certainly most business schools teach it as a stand-alone discipline with links to the CIPR. Leeds Business School has always had very close links with the CIPR and is deemed by many to be the leading PR higher education provider.

Some think PR leads a brand's comms and marketing activities, while others regard it as a key tool within the comms mix (Figure 2.1). Sadly, some see PR and marketing as oil and water – two disciplines divided by the same language, to paraphrase an old adage.

What do the marketers think of PR types?

According to the Chartered Institute of Marketing (CIM), PR can be defined as:

> [k]eeping good relations between a company or a group and the public so that people know what the company is doing and approve of it.
>
> *Dictionary of Marketing Terms*, 2003

Well, this is a nice enough start, if somewhat simplistic. How about PR is

> [t]he form of communication management that seeks to make use of publicity and other non-paid forms of promotion and information to influence the feelings, opinions, or beliefs about the company, its products or services, or about the value of the product or service or the activities of the organisation to buyers, prospects, or other stakeholders.
>
> *Dictionary of Marketing*, 2008

Again a pleasant enough definition that brings in the customers' perceptions of what you offer – which is, after all, what business is all about. The other stakeholders need a little more development, so how about: PR is a

> [c]onscious effort to improve and maintain an organisation's relationships with such publics as employees, customers,

shareholders, local communities, trade unions, with a view to strengthening reputation, ie building corporate image.

The CIM Marketing Directory, 1996

Now this is more like it. Marketers must consider the role of internal stakeholders and/or publics.

The idea of internal marketing (Figure 2.2) has long been discussed, and PR is a powerful tool for improving perceptions among your peers. It can counter misinformation and whispering campaigns, which are often based on gossip. As you know, a problem shared is a problem spread around the office! Some companies have taken draconian steps such as banning Facebook at work, purely with a view to controlling such internal 'noise'. Well, banning such tools can only be part of the solution, and stopping negativity is much easier when you have a positive message to fill the vacuum.

The reference to building relationships should chime with everyone as we all need to build relationships and not simply be transactional. We'll discuss this more in Chapter 6 when we consider PR as a tool for developing relationships with stakeholders through internal marketing.

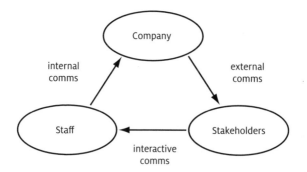
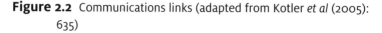

Figure 2.2 Communications links (adapted from Kotler *et al* (2005): 635)

Further to these definitions, the CIM website goes on to state that

Marketing is all about stakeholder communications, whether the stakeholders are customers, shareholders or employees of your organisation.

The phrase 'all about stakeholder communications' is the operative idea. Whether for someone who is predominantly a marketer or is predominantly a PR expert, this statement must ring true. The definition brings to the forefront the idea that PR is a key tool for communicating with your internal stakeholders.

So to answer the question, PR practitioners have the skills to provide solutions for, or with, marketers. The CIM has over 50,000 members worldwide. However, this is the tip of the (marketing) iceberg. Often these marketers are at board level and hold the budgets that PR agencies target, particularly in SMEs. Larger organisations often have directors of corporate communications, many of whom come from a PR background. Since marketing is 'all about stakeholder communications', then in truth PR practitioners and marketers are part of the same continuum and both serve the customer.

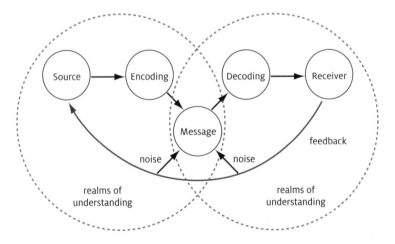

Figure 2.3 Model of communications (based on Schramm (1955) as cited in Shannon and Weaver (1962))

Always bear in mind that communication is a non-linear, continuous process (Figure 2.3). Why? Because as the world changes at what seems to be an increasing rate, the needs, wants and desires of our stakeholders and publics respond to these changes. Hence, so must our communication activities. Our messages need updating and, as stated earlier, technology has had a profound effect on this area of marketing. The nature and means of how we get our message to our receiver have never been more exciting with the options we now have available.

How do marketers use PR?

Well for a start, PR is more common than most people think. Let's consider a traditional marketing model to illustrate the usefulness of PR, namely the product life cycle (PLC) (Figure 2.4).

Every product is different, as is every PLC, and every new version of a product has a different PLC. Hence, the opportunities

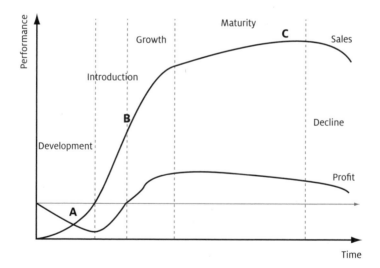

Figure 2.4 The generic product life cycle (PLC)

for PR are almost limitless, but let's consider the three scenarios depicted in Figure 2.4.

- *Zone A.* Your company is spending money developing and testing the product prior to release. Here you'd use press releases in publications relevant to your field. If it is a high-value product, you'd target top-of-the range magazines, possibly aiming to inform the early adopters. The campaign could be a teaser campaign or alternatively aimed at seeking input from opinion leaders and consumer leaders.
- *Zone B.* Your product has launched successfully and you want to extend the rapid growth so as to recoup more of your R&D costs. You may have set up social network sites and/or liaise with users' clubs. In either case, you'd seek testimonials explaining the benefits they've had from the products. You'd aim to feed positive feedback via the mass media as well as informing your customer base – that is, those clients who've so far held onto their old models. You could simply advertise. However, that's expensive and suffers from being 'marketer' dominant. That is, people expect you to say good things about your products but will gladly accept the word of real customers or other opinion formers.
- *Zone C.* You're seeking to extend the maturity section. Here you'd use PR to explain the reliability of your products. You'd recycle good feedback from magazines such as *Which?*, social network sites, user fora, comparison websites, and so on. If at all possible you'd want this to get into the mass media, so you may seek a new angle.

This principle of PR being a key tool for marketers is also evident in other models such as the diffusion-adoption curve and the new product development (NPD) process.

FAQ　Why do we need to know about opinion leaders and opinion formers?

People turn to others for support and guidance, therefore when you create your communications activities, you may reach others who are not the intended target. If they can influence the purchase, you need to draw them in so that they can support and ultimately influence the purchaser. The terms 'opinion formers' and 'opinion leaders' are what many marketers refer to when considering the communication process and the influence certain persons can have upon it.

An opinion former is somebody who, usually through their education and profession, has expertise to which you listen and respond. Think of it this way. If Toyota say, 'The new Toyota IQ is the best small car in the world', your reaction is usually muted as you expect them to say it (ie it's marketer-dominated information). If, however, Jeremy Clarkson of *Top Gear* fame says, 'The new Toyota IQ is the best small car in the world', the chances are that you'll listen to the message and (whether Jeremy denies it or not!) it will have more credibility. This is what we call non-marketer-dominated information and you trust it because Jeremy Clarkson is an opinion former or a maven. The reasons are as follows:

- **He has more knowledge in this area than you (or most people, for that matter).**
- **He has access to the latest cars and has test-driven more varieties than everyone you know put together.**
- **He is fiercely independent of the car manufacturer (as, by the way, is the magazine *Which?*).**

The combination of these attributes makes for a powerful communicator who can build trust and credibility for your brand. There's a risk, though, as you need to be confident that your product isn't going to be panned!

Opinion leaders have a social standing or closeness to us that lends their opinions credibility. Remember that a key *raison d'être* for your 'comms' is to support stakeholders, for example customers as they make purchase decisions, or colleagues who are going through changes... and yes, you'll have internal opinion formers as well as external, as we'll discuss in more detail in Chapter 6.

Summary and activities

Key points

Before you decide which communication tools to use to deliver your message from sender to receiver, there are a number of factors to consider that will help you choose the most appropriate communication tools, and indeed the configuration of the message you send.

Questions

1.   What does the term 'noise' mean?
2.   Why is communication a process and not linear?
3.   What is the difference between an opinion leader and an opinion former?

Activities

The CIM suggests the following, representing a small cross-section of PR websites that host a wealth of information:

- PR and Marketing Network (website: http://www. prandmarketing.com). For the latest news and strategies in US PR and marketing. You need to subscribe to access the archives.

- 10 Elements of an Effective Press Release (website: http://netpreneur.org/news/prmachine/pr/default.

html). Part of the Netpreneur Exchange. It includes a link to a sample press release.

- The Public Relations Society of America (website: http://www.prsa.org).

- *O'Dwyer's PR Daily* (website: http://www.odwyerpr. com). Good for breaking US PR news, opinion and archived articles. It also has a directory of PR companies, 'counsellors' and service companies.

- PR Museum (website: http://prmuseum.com). Has excellent profiles of US PR 'gurus', plus a bibliography of books held at the Museum Library regarding the history of PR.

- The International Association of Business Communicators (website: http://www.iabc.com). A professional network of more than 13,000 business communication professionals in over 60 countries.

- The International Public Relations Association (website: http://www.ipra.org). Has a directory of PR associations worldwide, plus summaries of conference papers, but you have to be a member to gain access.

3
Understanding strategic public relations

Planning your PR activities is fundamental to success. If you only do PR because you think you should, without understanding why you're doing it, you could be wasting valuable resources, including time and money.

All consumers' opinions on the products or services they have bought and used are formed by direct experience, word of mouth, reading reviews and engaging in online discussions. Companies seeking to identify and manage consumers' perceptions may use PR to build awareness and influence our opinions. It's not a coincidence that global brands like McDonald's, Google, Virgin and BMW generate opinions, whether consumers engage with their products or not. Sustained PR campaigns, combined with other marketing initiatives, ensure that these brands remain dominant and 'manage' their reputation while controlling messages being discussed by stakeholders. This involves strategic thinking, including investment in planning, implementation and evaluation.

FAQ Why is planning important?
PR is most effective when it is considered, planned and evaluated on an ongoing basis. You may make some errors on the way but

you'll learn from these and build on your experiences, ultimately making PR work well for you. While simply reacting to industry needs may reap short-term rewards, PR is more effective if the your company takes a lead – that is, is proactive. It's worth taking time to stop the daily PR activities (responding to journalists' requests, staff, community groups, etc) and question how you benefit by only reacting.

Stop reacting. Get focused and be strategic in your PR activities.

Identify opportunities and plan ways of engaging with them to make sure you're maximising positive outcomes. A company that:

- **isn't ready to respond to the media will soon fall out of favour with them, resulting in poor relations with journalists, resulting in weak or no coverage in the press;**
- **proactively engages with the media, getting to know what kind of stories they're looking for (and their deadlines), is going to be asked to give comments and gain more positive press coverage;**
- **fails to explain (to its staff) what is happening in the company, such as new structures, products, achievements and business concerns. will demoralise and disengage its workforce with subsequent ramifications, such as absenteeism and poor customer relations;**
- **engages with employees through consultation, newsletters, e-mail updates, events and meetings will produce motivated and positive employees who understand the value of good customer relations and are proud to represent their organisation.**

Planning your PR

So whether your plan is short term, based around a specific event, or a long-term programme of activities that affects the whole business, the same principles apply. Good planning will improve your understanding of why you're doing what you're doing. Planning allows you to:

- **focus on what matters and ensure that time isn't wasted on unnecessary activities;**
- **say no to unplanned activities and be able to justify why you're not prepared to spend time and effort on unnecessary activities;**
- **create cohesion in short-, medium- and long-term activities;**
- **reflect on current activities that will influence and impact on longer-term activities;**
- **be more cost-effective, as you'll be able to demonstrate past achievements to create effective programmes of activity in the future;**
- **engage all stakeholder groups in a timely manner by identifying their needs, and opportunities to contribute to your plan;**
- **work proactively and be in control of the agenda, allowing you to identify issues and opportunities and plan actions to address them.**

There are a number of key elements that must be considered before PR tactics are implemented. You must ask yourself:

- **What is it we want to achieve?**
- **Why do we want to do it?**
- **How, where and when are we going to do it?**
- **Who is going to do it?**
- **What is our budget?**

To address these elements it's wise to think strategically and adopt a plan (Figure 3.1), which we'll now discuss in more detail.

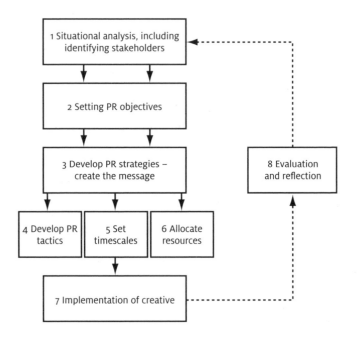

Figure 3.1 Strategic PR overview

Situation analysis, including identifying stakeholders (Stage 1)

In order to understand what needs addressing, you'll need to conduct a situational analysis by monitoring and understanding your external, uncontrollable environments (Figure 3.2). PESTEL is a widely used framework that you can use to conduct this analysis.

By monitoring your macro- and micro-environments objectively, you will better appreciate the challenges and opportunities available. This audit will enable you to develop a credible and effective PR plan based on clear objectives. It's best completed by an independent team who can provide input

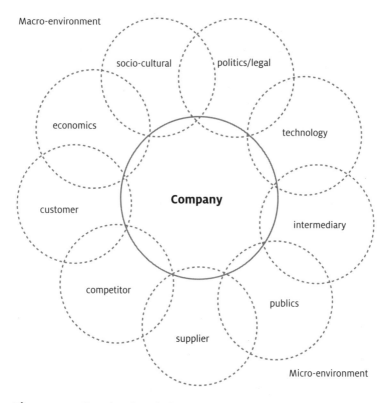

Figure 3.2 Situational analysis

effectively and quickly. Remember, all audits are inherently political, so the team will need support from the top.

Let's consider the PESTEL framework in more detail:

- *Political*: including areas such as tax policy, employment laws, environmental regulations, trade restrictions and reform, tariffs and political stability.
- *Economic*: economic growth or decline, interest rates, exchange rates and inflation rate, wage rates, minimum wage, working hours, unemployment (local and national), credit availability, cost of living, etc.

- *Socio-cultural*: cultural norms and expectations, health consciousness, population growth rate, age distribution, career attitudes, emphasis on safety, global warming.
- *Technological*: new technologies are continually being developed and the rate of change itself is increasing. Things that were not accessible until recently are now mainstream, eg mobile phone marketing, blogs, social networking websites.
- *Environmental* aspects: changing expectations, eg use of fuel, recycling, waste.
- *Legal*: may impact employment, access to materials, quotas, resources, imports/exports, taxation, etc.

Having carried out a thorough analysis of your macro-environment, you must also monitor your micro-environment to identify recent strengths and weaknesses with which you can address identified macro-opportunities and threats (Figure 3.3).

This illustrates how the components of the SWOT impact upon one another. Your analyses should produce a wealth of useful, detailed information (Figure 3.4).

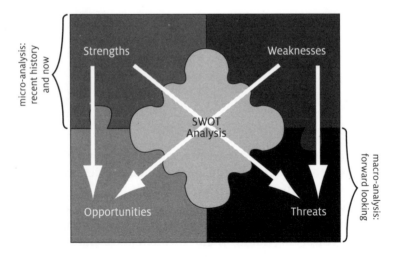

Figure 3.3 SWOT analysis showing how elements are interlinked

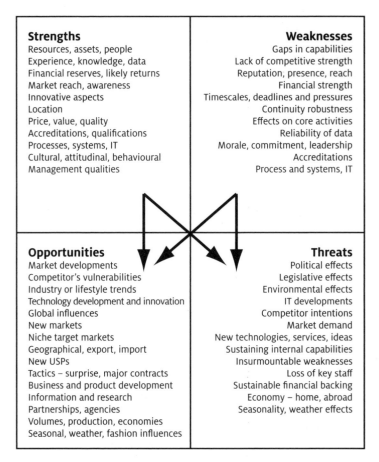

Strengths
Resources, assets, people
Experience, knowledge, data
Financial reserves, likely returns
Market reach, awareness
Innovative aspects
Location
Price, value, quality
Accreditations, qualifications
Processes, systems, IT
Cultural, attitudinal, behavioural
Management qualities

Weaknesses
Gaps in capabilities
Lack of competitive strength
Reputation, presence, reach
Financial strength
Timescales, deadlines and pressures
Continuity robustness
Effects on core activities
Reliability of data
Morale, commitment, leadership
Accreditations
Process and systems, IT

Opportunities
Market developments
Competitor's vulnerabilities
Industry or lifestyle trends
Technology development and innovation
Global influences
New markets
Niche target markets
Geographical, export, import
New USPs
Tactics – surprise, major contracts
Business and product development
Information and research
Partnerships, agencies
Volumes, production, economies
Seasonal, weather, fashion influences

Threats
Political effects
Legislative effects
Environmental effects
IT developments
Competitor intentions
Market demand
New technologies, services, ideas
Sustaining internal capabilities
Insurmountable weaknesses
Loss of key staff
Sustainable financial backing
Economy – home, abroad
Seasonality, weather effects

Figure 3.4 Populated SWOT analysis showing how elements interact

From Figure 3.4 you can start to see how the SWOT analysis could identify patterns and trends that will influence your PR programme. It can be used for strategic planning (eg acquisition opportunities, entering new markets, investment opportunities) or marketing planning (eg product development and launches, research). It can be from departmental or individual perspectives, looking at what you deliver to whom and how you do it. To be effective, it needs to be undertaken regularly as organisations that carry out regular SWOT analyses often spot trends before others, thus providing competitive advantage. It's worth remembering that SWOT analyses are snapshots at one specific time.

Analysis at this broad level will inform the direction you choose to work towards, helping to set clear objectives at corporate, campaign or project levels. PR may be one element used to help you fulfil your objectives at a corporate level, hence PR objectives must be aligned with corporate objectives. Many PR practitioners contribute to the bigger picture. This is when PR is at its most effective, fully integrated into the strategic direction of the organisation.

Setting PR objectives (Stage 2)

Identifying key objectives provides a platform and achievable goals for your PR activities; they are most effective if small in number, concise and SMART (Table 3.1).

Table 3.1 SMART objectives

Objective	Comments
Specific	Avoid being either too vague or too tightly focused.
Measurable	Always ensure you can measure the success of the objective.
Accurate (some say 'Aspirational' or 'Achievable')	Don't set a wish-list as nothing demotivates staff more quickly than imposed targets that can't be met.
Realistic	How probable is it that the objective will effect changes?
Timely (some say 'Targeted')	Depending on resources, identify the time when your objectives need may mean modifying, simplifying or being made more specific.

PR objectives are usually set at one of three levels:

1. *Raising awareness.* The family history website findmypast.com launched a service with The National Archives which made 36 million census records of people living in England and Wales in 1911 available online. Its PR objective was to generate public awareness of the launch of 1911census.co.uk.
2. *Altering attitudes and opinions. Collins English Dictionary* wanted to change the way dictionary editions are launched by showing that people, not academics, are able to create words that appear in the dictionary, hence making them more accessible to the general public.
3. *Changing behaviour.* The climate change charity Global Cool launched a PR drive to get more people to use public transport by targeting festival-goers.

Examples of PR objectives might include:

- **raising your profile;**
- **altering the attitudes and opinions of key stakeholders;**
- **increasing your market share.**

Developing PR strategies: creating the message (Stage 3)

Strategies are the broad methods chosen to achieve your objectives. They do not include details of courses of action that will be followed on a daily basis; these are tactics. It is important to understand what strategies are and how they differ from tactics.

Strategies can be derived from the SWOT analysis (Figure 3.4) in the form of a TOWS analysis (Table 3.2). Typical strategies could be:

- **SO1: raising your profile in the media by engaging more with journalists as part of a media campaign;**

Table 3.2 TOWS analysis

Strategies	Urgency	Probability	Impact	Total
SO1	3	3	3	9
SO2	3	3	2	8
SO3	3	2	3	8
WO1	2	2	2	6
WO2	2	2	1	5
WO3	2	2	1	5
ST1	3	2	3	8
ST2	2	2	2	6
ST3	2	1	1	4
WT1	2	2	1	5
WT2	2	1	1	4
WT3	1	1	1	3

- SO2: lobbying MPs to change the tax rates for small businesses;
- SO3: boosting product sales or service take-up, eg increase podcast downloads;

- ST: engaging more people in your online newsletter;
- ST2: educating your staff regarding new products;

- WT1: engaging in research that will allow you to use your strengths to counter weaknesses;
- WT2: developing a social media campaign to target hitherto unreachable youth segments.

Key messages

Every PR campaign or strategy needs a set of messages that convey the main focus of the communication. They will help to inform and influence opinion, so must be clear, concise and easily understood. When deciding what your messages should say, you must first identify your target audience. This will determine how technical or simple the messages should be. You may be required to develop a suite of messages to suit a range of different audiences. In each case the underlying message will be similar or the same, just said in a different way to appeal to the relevant audiences.

Messages must also be highly credible, and are often delivered alongside advertising to reinforce the messages. Any hint of verbose claims or badly researched statistics will damage the credibility of the message and the overall campaign, and subsequently your reputation.

Sub-messages can be used to reinforce the main message. For example, Tesco's 'Every little helps' message is reinforced with product-line messages on value; Marks & Spencer's message on quality is reinforced with product-line messages on quality.

Consideration must also be made on how to present the message. What tone, context and format you choose will each impact on how the message is interpreted. You won't be able to control all of these elements but should consider them as part of your situational analysis.

Example
In spring 2009, Waitrose advertised its 'branded products', which are 'value' products in consideration of the public mood during the credit crunch. This advertising message was reinforced with articles in the press about Waitrose's range of value products. Similarly, the car industry is attempting to appeal to the environmentally conscious public with ranges of 'fuel-efficient' vehicles.

Developing PR tactics (Stage 4)

The strategy is 'how' you will achieve your objectives. Having a clear strategy will keep the tactics focused on a particular area such as media relations, internal communications, social media or community relations. The tactics may have been tried and tested or create an opportunity to experiment within a focused environment.

Messages must be credible and able to match your levels of persuasion as identified in your objective setting. You must consider the following:

- *Format.* **Consider how messages are to be delivered – using words, songs, slogans, photos or images? What font and size? They must fit your overall identity and existing profile, unless you are undertaking a radical relaunch.**
- *Tone and context.* **Adopt an appropriate mood, which, depending on your audience, may be upbeat or sombre. It may reflect the general mood of the nation. For example, in a recession, banks are showing restraint by sending out messages about safe investments, rather than encouraging people to take out irresponsibly large loans.**
- *Newsworthiness.* **Your messages must communicate something worthwhile and of benefit to your audience. What may interest you (say a message full of jargon) may not be appropriate to a mainstream audience, but may be suitable for a trade or technical audience, including clients, suppliers, investors and the like.**

Developing tactics could be considered as the creative, fun part of the planning process and implementation. Indeed, many PRs' reputations are gained from the success of their creative ideas and tactics. The key question to ask, once you've established your aims and objectives, is 'What are we going to do to achieve them?' Your strategy might identify the need for a media campaign, but 'what are we actually going to do?' to achieve a successful media campaign involves developing tactics.

Basing tactics on a media campaign – for example, where you are going to increase your coverage in trade publications or the quality newspapers – involves asking yourself a series of questions:

- **What can we do to stand out from our competitors so journalists will notice us?**
- **Is a simple press release enough or does it need some sort of gimmick, incentive or product sample to go with it?**
- **Who are the journalists we want to target and why?**
- **How are we going to contact them?**
- **What shall we do to make sure they have received and understood our message?**

Setting timescales (Stage 5)

Consider the events surrounding your messages. For example, if you're launching a campaign with messages of festive cheer via the media, you'll need to be know when to send them as monthly publications have a three-month lead-in and come out the month prior to their dated publication. By August it may be too late to send out messages of Christmas cheer via monthly magazines, but it will be too early for weekly and daily publications.

Allocating resources (Stage 6)

If you don't have a dedicated PR practitioner in your organisation, you'll need to identify who is going to implement and monitor the strategy. Maybe you're confident enough to have a go yourself, or you could use existing staff within marketing, sales or broader communications roles.

An alternative is to speak to local or national PR agencies, depending on your sector. Many companies work with agencies because of their good contacts with the press, or their understanding of specific sectors or industry knowledge. In Chapter 10 we'll discuss PR costs further.

Implementing the creative (Stage 7)

You must know your audience – that is, at whom you're aiming your messages. This might include different stakeholder groups from customers (existing and potential), investors, competitors, staff, local communities, trade unions and decision-makers such as MPs, councillors and professional bodies. Stakeholder mapping is regularly used to identify different groups of individuals who form your stakeholder profile. You need to consider who has, and who might have, influence and power over your business and objectives.

Many companies rightly focus much time and effort on customers. However, PR covers a broad range of stakeholders, including groups who are 'dormant', 'active' and 'passive'. The role of engagement with these groups may change and evolve, depending on both your and their activities. If your business wants to expand its premises, it will need to consider not only existing customers but also your staff and the communities you might impact on with building development, as well as town planners and councillors (discussed in more detail in Chapter 6).

Evaluation and reflection (Stage 8)

You must understand the benefit of your PR activities, and hence your investment of time and money must be evaluated to ensure that you're achieving your PR objectives and that your strategies and tactics are effective. In Chapter 10 we'll discuss costs and evaluation in more detail. However, the following examples provide insights into evaluation and how to conduct it effectively. You'll notice there's a value to the PR activity that has taken place that's based on how much it would cost to advertise in the publications that featured the free coverage.

Example 1: 'The pigs are worth it'

Objective: To save the British pig industry following a disastrous wheat harvest that meant pig farmers faced high feed prices and crippling losses.

Strategy: To reflect the very high standards of animal welfare in British pig farming, the crisis the industry faced and to put pressure on supermarkets to raise the price they paid for pigs via a PR-led campaign that included lobbying the relevant minister and the public.

Tactics: Activities ranged from a report into the effect of feed prices, to pig farmers recording an anthem. The 'Pig-o-meter Tour' featured a giant pig counting farmers' mounting losses, and a rally on Downing Street involving hundreds of farmers. 'Winnie the Pig' culminated in the presentation of a 13,000-signature petition. Media backing underpinned widespread support from MPs. There was a London Underground poster campaign. A report on high feed prices was presented to journalists and MPs. The report *Is the Government Buying British?* called on the public sector to buy British. There was a 'Celebrity chefs "choose pork"' promotion, with trade publication coverage to put pressure on retailers. There was support from Jamie Oliver with the Channel 4 documentary *Jamie Saves Our Bacon* in January 2009.

Evaluation: The price paid for pigs rose from £1.06 per kilogram to the target £1.40 per kilogram, with consumer purchases remaining strong. This amounted to an extra £5.1 million per week for the industry. The campaign reached an audience of 104 million through the print media coverage alone and an additional 18.6 hours of television and radio coverage. The government established a 'Pig Industry Task Force'.

Example 2: Relaunch of football pools by Sportech
Objective: To relaunch the 85-year-old brand, communicate the social responsibility message of £1.1 billion donated by the organisation to the arts and good causes
Strategy: To reach to a new mainstream using a media campaign that brought the arts and football together.
Tactics: Teamed up with English National Ballet, who choreographed and performed *The Beautiful Game*, which was showcased to the media following a poll by fans of the top 10 iconic moments of football history. More than 20,000 football fans took part in the poll, via The New Football Pools website, which was also seeded or linked into 180 websites, fan sites, blogs and online forums.
Evaluation: Sportech reported a 39 per cent increase in full-year profit for 2008 due to the relaunch activity. Over 100 pieces of coverage, including spreads in five national newspapers, with a media value of £1.1 million.

Summary and activities

Key points

- You must continuously monitor your macro- and micro-environments in order to identify patterns and trends that will influence your PR programme.
- Use PR to engage your employees through consultation, newsletters, e-mail updates, events and meetings; they'll be more likely to achieve competitive advantage via increased customer satisfaction.
- Good planning will help you to understand why you are doing what you are doing, whether you are involved with short- or long-term PR programmes.
- Every PR campaign or strategy needs a set of messages that convey the main focus of the communication. The

strategy is 'how' you will achieve your objectives. Tactics should be closely linked to the strategy. Having a clear strategy will keep the tactics focused on a particular area.

- Having a set of clear messages aligned with the corporate or campaign objectives will also help to evaluate the success objectives. Measuring media coverage in relation to whether the key messages are being or were conveyed is a great way to determine success. A set of vague or numerous messages may result in vague results.

Questions

1. What are the factors in the macro-environment?
2. Identify the parties that create your micro-environment.
3. Why is the micro-environment partly controllable?
4. Why monitor the macro-environment?

Activities

Always look at the BBC website (http://www.bbc.co.uk) and the national broadsheet newspapers (eg www.timesonline.co.uk) to keep an eye on movements in the environment. Reading magazines/books/articles such as *The Economist* (http://www.economist.com) is also helpful.

4

Working with the media

Anyone who regularly reads or listens to the news will be aware that it's a bit like storytelling in a very restricted amount of time. The biggest challenge in working with the media is understanding what makes a news story and how to communicate it to journalists. For many PR practitioners, media relations and writing for the media is the main focus of their work, taking up most their time. Much effort goes into developing good relationships with journalists. Media relations is highly valued as a PR tool because of its impartiality; journalists are largely impartial and objective, they look at a story from all angles and generally their reporting is considered to be factual and credible.

For companies wanting to be featured in newspapers, trade publications, radio or television and, increasingly, online news pages, the two main options are to pay for advertising or to generate free coverage through PR or media relations.

Advertising

Advertising may be regarded as 'pay to play' and PR as 'pray to play'. Advertising involves guaranteed placement, using the words

and images supplied by the individual or organisation that is
paying for the advert.

Media relations

PR involves working with journalists to generate news items
that are verified and edited by journalists. Journalists usually
write the news article based on a news release or news story that
may require further investigation and is usually more
considered, more objective and written by a third party, lacking
in biased information. The placement of the news item in this
form is free.

As more of us get our news online and watch delayed TV,
merrily skipping adverts, more companies are switching from
advertising to PR. The public have grown up with advertising and
are increasingly cynical about the messages they receive via
adverts. Today's public are more inclined to trust words written by
a journalist.

The media

Newspapers and consumer magazines

Journalists are very busy, working to tight deadlines in an
increasingly challenging environment with many newspapers
experiencing declining sales and readership. The internet is the
main challenger to the newspaper industry; as soon as a
newspaper is printed, many of its news stories are out of date.
They are increasingly becoming opinion papers, with journalists
commenting on the news rather than 'breaking' the news.
However, they are still influential and many have invested heavily
in their online news websites, which are increasingly interactive
and dependent on 'citizen journalism', with the public often
reporting the news as it happens.

Trade publications

Trade newspapers, of which there are thousands, include weekly, fortnightly, monthly and quarterly magazines and specialise in a particular subject, sector or trade. Whether your business supplies pigeon feed to pigeon fanciers, nuts and bolts to the building trade or hair products to supermarkets, there'll be a trade publication for you. It will be supplied to and read by your target audience, customers and prospects alike, reporting industry news and developments, new entrants or alternatively businesses in decline. It will report on industry trends and opinion leaders' views on the future, and will generally provide a forum to review and report on what matters to its readers, who are its key stakeholders.

Television and radio

'Broadcast' media offers a variety of opportunities for publicity, from daytime chat shows to current affairs news programmes and a range of options in between. The huge number of different programmes on radio and television available through satellite and cable channels, as well as more specialist programmes, means these options should be targeted carefully. Consideration must be given to the 'lead-in time', meaning how much notice is required by editors for the development of programmes, and to how the programme makers gather their content. Most news channels, for example, will have a forward features desk with events and dates pencilled in well in advance, but there's always the opportunity for more current news to 'bump' or 'push' these features off the agenda. A phone call to the news editor is advisable. For example, for a 6 pm TV news programme the news agenda will often be decided at a morning planning meeting, so put a call in early to make sure your news item is discussed.

How to gain media coverage

News releases

Most journalists receive hundreds of e-mails daily containing 'news stories' or news releases. Many are full of grammatical and spelling errors, while others lack relevance for the media outlet or region they target, or simply are not newsworthy. Yet despite the challenges journalists face in dealing with huge numbers of news releases, they offer the most effective way to get media coverage for your company.

A news release should not be any longer 300 words, with any supplementary information being placed at the end of the release. A clear heading should explain to a journalist succinctly what the main theme of the story is, for example 'Barack Obama voted first black US president'.

The first paragraph should contain the main elements of the story – the five Ws: who, what, where, when and why as well as how. If all these elements are relevant, the journalist should be able to answer them via a combination of the headline and the first paragraph. Supporting information will then be contained within the remaining text. PR practitioners refer to the 'inverted pyramid' (Figure 4.1) to help identify and prioritise the crucial elements of a news release.

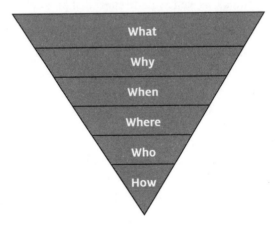

Figure 4.1 Inverted pyramid

Testing the five Ws

The following details a headline and opening paragraph for a variety of news releases issued by recognised brands:

Example 1: Olympic Park opens its doors to 4,000 Londoners for Open House Weekend
11 August 2009   The Olympic Delivery Authority (ODA) is aiming to break last year's record number of visitors to the Olympic Park as part of Open House London, the capital's largest architectural showcase.

Example 2: HSBC raises stake in Bank Ekonomi to over 98 per cent
HSBC has completed a mandatory tender offer (MTO) for the remaining 10.11 per cent of the shares of PT Bank Ekonomi Raharja Tbk (Bank Ekonomi).

Example 3: Over 500 voluntary organisations helped through the recession by £15 million fund
Today, 26 Aug 2009, 558 frontline charities and voluntary organisations across the country will receive grants worth up to £40,000 to help them provide vital community services during the recession.

News is about human interest

Most news stories have a human interest element, especially those used in the consumer media. Give your release a human element by including quotes or include a human angle by including a relevant experience of, say, a customer, employee or MD/CEO. You may want to include more than one quote, which is quite common, but any words you add to a release, whether in the general copy or attributed to an individual, must add to the news element. Do not simply repeat within a quote what you've already said in the main body of the release.

When using quotes, make sure you have the permission of the quoted individual. They'll want to see what you've attributed to them or may want to write it themselves. It's also important that the person quoted in a news release is available to talk to the press in case the press want to verify the quote or gain some further information from them.

Using bullet points or diagrams can be useful to present information more succinctly and also help to break up the paragraphs of a release. Note that news releases:

- **must be brief and well written;**
- **unlike most storytelling, start with the conclusion;**
- **must contain a clear title, date and contact information of the sender, including e-mail address and phone number;**
- **use quotations to give a human interest angle;**
- **use bullet points or diagrams to display information effectively;**
- **must be checked for errors before sending.**

Practical hints and tips

Structure of a news release
The following represents a typical news release:

- **Date: current – even yesterday is dated!**
- **clear heading – factual, not too creative;**
- **tense: present tense – is rather than has;**
- **200–300 words, double line-spaced;**
- **quotation in third or fourth paragraph;**
- **short paragraphs with short, sharp sentences;**
- **clear 'end' of news release;**
- **clear named contact details;**
- **further notes to editor.**

Five things you should not do
Figure 4.2 summarises common key mistakes that you should avoid. Let's discuss these in more detail:

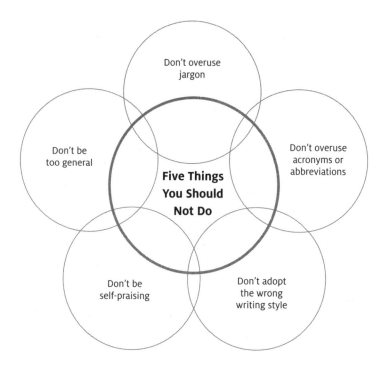

Figure 4.2 Five things you should not do

- Don't overuse jargon, except perhaps in small-circulation academic, scientific or industry journals that have very exclusive readerships. The use of jargon should be avoided as it prevents understanding.
- Don't overuse acronyms or abbreviations. Use them only where they are essential. They must always be written in full the first time they are used unless they are so commonplace that their meaning will be immediately understood, for example MP, CEO.
- Don't adopt the wrong writing style. Releases, case studies, features, reports and trade literature all have characteristic writing styles. Copy length, tone and presentation must fit the style of communication.

- **Don't be too general.** Copy written for a general audience cannot appeal to personal experience and will not retain the attention or engage the thoughts of readers.
- **Don't be self-praising.** Copy that is heavy on adjectives and self-praise often creates the opposite impression because of its lack of substance and credibility.

Feature articles

Most printed publications run feature articles as well as news articles. Often written by PR people in conjunction with journalists, feature articles are longer than news releases. They vary from 500 to 1,500 words and usually involve more comment and opinion as well as being accompanied by photographs or other visual aids. They are often more considered than a news item, so it's advisable to discuss the development of a feature article with a journalist in advance. Features are usually exclusively written for a target audience via one media outlet, for example a trade magazine or a particular national or regional newspaper.

Phone or e-mail a journalist?

How are you going to make sure the journalist reads your news release? Writing a news release can be the easy part; targeting it effectively so you get some coverage is more challenging.

As news releases are usually included in the main body of e-mails to journalists rather than as attachments, they must be brief and written effectively. It's important that your release stands out with an attention-grabbing headline in the e-mail title to entice them to open your e-mail. More important still, make sure you target your release to the correct journalist. As well as a general news desk, most media outlets have journalists working on specialist areas such as business, science, education, health, features and sport, to name but a few. It is worth becoming very familiar with the format, and names of journalists who will be most interested in your area of business.

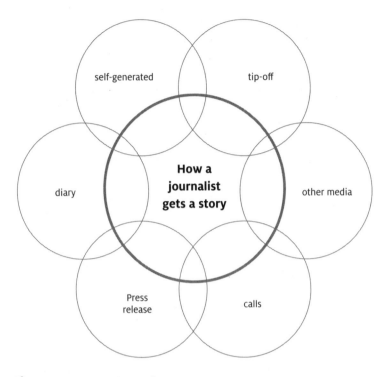

Figure 4.3 How a journalist gets a story

Building relationships with journalists is a good investment of your time as it will maximise opportunities of media coverage. Most journalists will welcome a phone call to introduce yourself or your organisation. If they're busy with deadlines, they'll usually tell you so and suggest a better time to call. They may also welcome the opportunity to meet you, either formally or informally to discuss how you can contribute to their news gathering.

Once you have made these contacts and built these relationships, it can be beneficial to have a chat with your contact to discuss up-and-coming news items in advance of sending or even writing a news release. You can ask their opinion as to what is most likely to be covered and they will advise on what you should focus on in order to maximise your coverage.

It is always worth considering what else is being discussed in the news, what's topical! Can your company or colleagues comment on national or regional issues, or can they bring a regional angle to a national story? Remember, journalists may be busy on other news stories, in which case don't waste your story. Save it until it's more appropriate.

Timing of video and audio news releases

If it's the day of the Chancellor's Budget announcements, don't send a release or call a journalist with a story that isn't relevant to this important event. Your item may not be of any interest to the journalist and it may get lost among the bigger story. It may not gain any coverage at all or be reduced to a NIB (news in brief).

Whom to target?

Most SMEs will have a news publication that they'll aspire to be featured in; this could be the regional or local newspaper, a trade publication or a business magazine. The most effective way to get your company featured is to understand what the journalists are seeking, what sort of stories they write about, what writing style they use and how frequently the publication appears.

Example
Netto saw 6.6 per cent growth between August 2007 and August 2009. It overcame its discount image of a store stocked with unexciting, unfamiliar European products. The store targeted journalists on consumer magazines and national newspapers with new products and requested that the store be referred to as a 'supermarket' rather than a discount store. New stores were opened, with special events

to attract local shoppers. Consumers were educated to view Netto as a contender to the established supermarkets via targeted PR activities.

What to say?

Having identified your target publication, you must consider what you want to say. Keep it simple! Don't overcomplicate things by trying to say too much; one or two key messages are most appropriate. Most news articles are of fewer than 250 words and aimed at audiences with far less knowledge of your product or service than you, so make sure you use appropriate language. The use of technical words and phrases might be appropriate for a trade publication but considered as jargon and over-complicated if targeted at the regional newspapers.

How to say it?

Reading the publications that you want to feature in will help you to understand what sort of stories are featured, how long the items tend to be, how frequently the publication is printed, what sort of variety of articles are usually featured and any special features that are coming up that you might want to contribute to or comment on.

Ask yourself questions like: What will the readers already know? How much background information do I need to supply to help them understand the value of the story? How long will they be prepared to spend reading my story?

When to say it?

If a publication is printed daily, then it's essential that you understand the deadlines a journalist might be working towards and when he or she will be most receptive to your e-mail or phone call. For weekly, monthly and quarterly publications it's advisable to speak to journalists and find out what their deadlines are.

Whom to say it to?

Most journalists like to receive information by e-mail, although it is a challenge to make sure your e-mail is read by them, because of the large volume they receive every day. A way to overcome this is to ring them in advance to let them know you are sending them an e-mail. Take this opportunity to discuss the content of your story with them and to check they'll be happy to receive it. They may advise you to send it to a specific journalist or ask for some key bits of information to be included, such as a quotation from a named person in the company or a photograph to go with the story.

Why are you saying it?

A news release must be relevant and current to the reader. Newspapers survive on being able to target stories appropriately to their audiences and they are dependent on receiving a good supply of information in order to maintain their edge over their competitors. Stories must include elements of news or surprise as they must inform and enlighten the reader. Reflecting on the value of your news story is very important, and it's always better to wait until you really have some news rather than sending regular news releases.

Use of photography and images

You can maximise the impact of your news release by illustrating it with images or photographs. Take a good look at the publication you want to feature in; what sort of images does it use, how are photos or images used?

Most readers of news publications glance at the photo and headline before deciding whether the article is worth reading, so make your photos stand out! A good photo or image can mean your story is featured in a more prominent place within the publication. Readers' attention will be drawn towards a photo story within the first three pages and in a central position or at the top right hand of the page, rather than as a NIB. NIBs are the short articles with no images, featured in a column down the left- or right-hand side of the page.

Many companies have a selection of stock images which they may use regularly to go with news stories, or they may commission a set of photographs to go with a specific story. The key is to make the photo illustrate the story accurately and creatively.

Before you send a journalist a photograph, make sure he or she has the capacity to receive it; the journalist may ask you to send it directly to the 'picture desk'. You must make sure the photo can be identified. Give it the same name as your news release, and provide a list, from left to right, of the individuals in the photos. Check that their names are spelled correctly!

Dos and don'ts for photography

Let's now consider some best practices and typical pitfalls.

Further to the pitfalls (Table 4.1), don't fall foul of the 'lamp-post effect' in which respected managers are unwittingly turned into comedy figures with antennae coming out of the tops of their heads. Also try to avoid the 'James Purnell' effect; he was famously Photoshopped into a photo after he missed an official NHS photoshoot in Manchester in 2007. It looks tacky and very obvious when you try to amend or alter images in this way – not to mention being a PR own goal, as the press made hay at the time.

Table 4.1 Dos and don'ts

Dos
• Think about who and what you want to feature in the photo.
• Consider the backdrop carefully. Office shots can be boring; logos and backdrops can be over the top and more appropriate for advertising material than news stories.
• Make the photo as interactive and relevant as possible. Have people doing something relevant to the story rather than simply posing.
• Consider paying a professional photographer to take the photo; they usually have an hourly charge, so it's worth getting a variety of photos taken to make it worthwhile.
• Negotiate standard hourly charges for photographers. These can range from £100 for general professional photographers to several thousand pounds for specialist photographers.
• Ask what else the photographs could be used for, such as your website, corporate literature and publications, promotional materials, exhibition displays, posters and recoil stands for events or the reception area.
• Make the photo work hard for you!

Don'ts
• Don't have too many people in the photo; three is usually sufficient.
• Don't try to please everyone who might want to be in the photo. You can always have a group photo at the end of the photoshoot to please those who feel they should be included and perhaps include these images in corporate literature or on the intranet or website.
• Don't have people standing in a line, handing over a cheque or certificate. Photos like this are banned from most publications as too hammy, and they look very dull.
• Don't take photos inside if they could be taken outside. Most photos come out better if set up outside where the lighting is usually better, so be flexible. Have your photos taken outside if possible but inside if the weather is unsuitable.
• Don't take photos of people sitting behind a desk. Again these are very dull.
• Don't have a backdrop that lets down the photo. Consider the surroundings carefully.

Working with celebrities

As the media and the public continue to be intrigued by 'celebrities' and the consumer magazines continue to thrive, many companies are using celebrities to promote their products or services. This approach can work well for many brands, especially if there is a real synergy between brand and celebrity.

Example 1
Outdoor retailer Berghaus opened its first retail store in September 2007 with explorer Sir Chris Bonington abseiling and unzipping two pieces of branded fabric covering the store frontage, revealing it to the crowd. While this created an exciting opportunity for the shoppers, it primarily provided a great photo-opportunity for the media, and the story was used widely in the press, with 'higher than expected' footfall in the store as well as increased takings recorded in the first month.

Example 2
The Meningitis Research Foundation has a number of high-profile celebrities who act as patrons, including the actor Ewan McGregor, James Dyson, TV doctor Hilary Jones, soccer legend Pat Jennings, and David and Victoria Beckham. Patrons agree to support the charity and get involved in fundraising activities and promotions. All of these celebrities will have a good understanding of the condition from personal contact with those affected by meningitis. Victoria Beckham contracted viral meningitis in 2000.

Example 3
Sir Clive Woodward helped Johnson and Johnson Vision Care promote eye testing with its Hero Campaign for Hero Brands

awareness campaign, which aimed to spread the message that an eye examination can help people perform 'to the best of their ability'. The company also did a TV tour with heptathlete Kelly Sotherton and a radio tour with mixed doubles badminton pair Gail Emms and Nathan Robertson. The campaign was covered by the BBC programme *Breakfast*, Sky News, *The Times*, the *Daily Mail*, the *Daily Telegraph*, *The Guardian*, *Metro*, Eurosport and Setanta. The magazine *Optician* reported a 4 per cent annual rise in eye tests in 2008.

Example 4
Shelter Scotland lobbied the Scottish administration and generated a 'gift for journalists on a tabloid paper' when it developed a campaign fronted by bands Idlewild and the Wombats to encourage 18- to 24-year-olds to press for the enforcement of legislation that every homeless person in Scotland will have the right to a permanent home by 2012.

This celebrity culture has provided a healthy income for celebrities from all walks of life; contenders on *Dragons' Den*, *Big Brother* and other reality TV shows are used to promote a range of businesses and products as well as speak at events. Their degree of success affects how much they charge. Expect to pay anything from their train fare to a photoshoot to £30,000 for their involvement in endorsing your brand.

If you can build a relationship with these individuals and create a real synergy with them, you should be able to find a celebrity who will recognise the opportunities that their contribution makes to your organisation and their reputation without your having to pay too much for their services.

Celebrity endorsement can also damage your reputation, and organisations must be quick to back away from a celebrity who might bring them into disrepute by association. A drunk sportsperson, a cocaine-snorting model or an actor swearing publicly can quickly become headline news for all the wrong reasons, so you must make sure your celebrity has a squeaky-clean record and no skeletons in the closet!

Summary and activities

Key points

- The biggest challenge to working with the media is understanding what makes a news story and how to communicate it to journalists.
- Journalists are busy people who work to tight deadlines in an increasingly challenging environment. However, they offer the most effective way to get coverage for your company in the media.
- Most news stories, particularly those in the consumer media, include human interest elements by incorporating one or more quotes, or a human angle such as customer or employee experiences.

Questions

1. What are the key elements that help to make up a news release?
2. How would you approach the media to cover your story?
3. What sort of visuals help to make a good story great?

Activities

When you're reading the newspaper, distinguish between news articles and feature articles. See whether you can spot which news articles are driven by a news release. Test this out by taking a look at the websites of those detailed in the article to see whether there is a press release to match with the newspaper article. It may not be exactly the same but it may have prompted the article.

Vary the newspapers and news websites you read so you can get a feel for the types of articles that appear to appeal to different audiences.

Explore how many trade publications are relevant to your sector and which ones most fit your line of business. Read them on a regular basis and identify key journalists you might like to target with a news release.

Look critically at the photographs that accompany news articles. Can you spot why they have been used? Do they tell the story without your having to read the article?

Take a look at some FTSE 100 companies or competitors in your sector to see what sort of media relations they are engaging in. Most will have a press or media website from their homepage website.

5

PR and developments in online communications

The internet, especially Web 2.0, has revolutionised how companies communicate with stakeholders. Websites are not like 'brochures' any more; they're about engagement and constantly develop to ensure visitors are kept interested. Their reach and ability to be personalised mean that those who have recognised the potential are busy engaging with global communities.

The newspaper industry was among the first industries to appreciate the benefits of the social media era. Nowadays, companies are increasingly utilising online PR activities via blogs and social media sites, such as Facebook, LinkedIn and Twitter. Engaging with stakeholders via interactive websites generates feedback and consumer contributions via discussions that may influence their brand choices. While there is a definite set of 'most popular' social media sites, we don't know what tomorrow's technology or 'fad' may be – but we do know that companies which do not engage with stakeholders online risk being discussed on social networking sites for all the wrong reasons.

Managing your reputation online

The risks associated with a lack of online engagement include publics discussing your brand in a negative way, which may gather pace, attracting large global audiences and ultimately damaging your brand. It's impossible to stop people talking about your brand. Indeed, it could be just the sort of positive PR you require, but in order to maximise it you must monitor and contribute to discussions, correcting errors and acting on feedback, both good and bad. It can take companies many years to build reputations that can be destroyed in minutes by disgruntled bloggers. Managing your reputation online is essential to protecting your brand and business from criticism and scrutiny.

In 2007, Google added blogs to its search engine criteria. Blogs allow users to write web pages and make them available to the public. Some companies have internal blogs or member-only blogs. There are millions of blogs that have been created by people who understand that with a bare minimum of knowledge they can make any information or view public. Most blogs allow readers to add comments to their blog 'posting'. Blogs are updated more regularly than websites, hence when someone 'Googles' a subject, the websites that appear on the first page are usually a selection of weblogs. Subsequently, any disgruntled clients who 'blog' about your business will come higher in Google searches than your own 'static' website. This encourages others to enter these blogs before they enter your site, especially if they are looking for reviews, hence the seeds of damage have been sown. Prospects who read bad reviews may avoid purchasing your products or services.

Maximising your reach

You'll seek to maximise your Google ranking to draw consumers to your site. This requires regular editing of your site, linking it to other sites, including blogs and social network sites. The resulting increase in 'hits' raises your Google ranking. The most obvious way to manage your online reputation is to Google your name, website name or product name frequently, making sure that nothing undesirable appears. Use online tools like Google Alerts to automate this process. Constantly enhancing and updating your website, developing links to other active social sites, will see your address increasingly embedded in a range of sites, and so the links grow, as do the opportunities to reach new audiences. Remember, you must maintain your Google ranking by updating and interacting with such sites regularly.

The power of bloggers

Transparency is crucial in order to be credible and earn respect. Some PR practitioners have rightly been criticised by internet users for contributing to online discussions that support their products or clients without declaring their interest. This is seen as unethical behaviour by the CIPR. Customer feedback is highly desirable and you must engage in these relationships in sincere, transparent and consistent ways. If you come across unwanted negative comments, you must act quickly and professionally. Engage with the blogger, either by e-mail or by responding to their blog online. Customers will forgive isolated failings and respect companies that learn from these incidences.

Example

Virgin didn't react quickly enough to a disgruntled blogger whose comments on his in-flight cuisine became an overnight hit, owing to the blog's witty and engaging style. It took just two days for it to feature in printed and online news outlets. Finally, Richard Branson responded in person to the individual, congratulating him on his blogging success and inviting him to advise on the company's in-flight menus.

The key is to respond quickly, address the situation, apologise if necessary and, above all, prevent it from becoming the lead story in the news for all the wrong reasons.

Microblogs

A microblog is modelled on a blog but allows only very limited space for writing a message. These messages can be followed both online and via mobiles. Twitter, launched in July 2006, allows signed-up members to write comments up to 120 characters long. Social networking sites like Facebook are remodelling themselves on this popular development and allowing members to update regularly with short comments or 'status updates'.

Example 1
News of the US Airways passenger plane crash into the Hudson River in New York in January 2009 was communicated around the world in real time more quickly than any news channel could keep up, as a witness to the crash recorded the incident and updated his 'Twitter' page, sending pictures and news of the crash around the world in seconds.

Example 2
Sheffield International Venues successfully uses Twitter to update its clients on class changes, opening times and unforeseen occurrences that mean its leisure centres have to close (because of flooding, electrical faults, etc). When one centre was recently closed owing to an electrical failure, clients were able to go straight home without the inconvenience of parking at the centre or getting stuck in traffic or becoming frustrated at the centre, demonstrating the immense value of immediate communication to its customers.

Really Simple Syndication (RSS)

Web users frequently sign up to receive information from selected blogs, social websites or public websites by clicking on the RSS link on relevant pages. News websites provide RSS feeds so that viewers can receive automatic updates on selected topics. This is a great way for PR practitioners to follow information on their industry, sector and even company or organisation.

> **Example**
> Neil regularly uses an RSS site to follow the ups and downs of his beloved football team (website: http://www.newsnow. co.uk/h/Sport/Football/Premier+League/Sunderland). It offers a useful insight on how stories often have different takes in the global media, as well as often providing entertaining comments from supporters.

New media release

News releases have adapted to the online environment and evolved into 'new media releases' that are e-mailed to journalists for use in online and printed publications. The new media release is complete with live links (hyperlinks), RSS feeds, photographs, videos and other social media.

Pay per clicks

The online advertising opportunity offered by pay per clicks is the fastest-growing form of advertising worldwide. Companies that place advertisements within websites are charged for the number of clicks on the advert. Pay per clicks can also be used as a PR tool to encourage clicks onto your website or key message, and can be easily monitored (using readily available software) and evaluated.

Search engine optimisation (SEO)

Many companies invest time and energy into enhancing their position in the listings that search engines produce. When people seek new sites, they'll enter key words into the search engines, usually Google, Yahoo! or MSN. Search engines continuously develop and constantly monitor popular sites that fit the key words. The opportunity to maximise search rankings has led to a strong growth in SEO agencies, or search marketing agencies, which use a combination of good copy (written words) and strong technical IT skills.

> **Example**
> Numbering an estimated 175 million, worldwide retailers' websites are among the most visited. Tesco is ranked 32 and BT at 39 in the world, with billions of online interactions, far more than any high street outlet could cope with, making the online marketplace the most economically efficient in the world.

How PR uses social media

The main changes affecting PR are the speed, transparency and interaction of modern communications. What you may have previously discussed with journalists is now available to everyone at the click of a button, including customers, competitors, staff and other stakeholder groups. Companies that depended on static websites are now upgrading them to offer visitors much more interaction and entertainment. Rather than being merely a repository of information, Web 2.0 allows discussion and the adding and sharing of information. It is taking the concept of e-mail, original websites and message boards and putting them together into one central site that is more efficient, effective and essential to many developing businesses.

Many PR practitioners are harnessing this opportunity and making it work for their clients, using a combination of RSS feeds, embedded links to and from websites, updating microsites and social media sites. All of these activities direct 'traffic' to and from relevant websites that aim to develop two-way communication with stakeholders.

The Long Tail of PR

The Long Tail of PR is a way to demonstrate that the use of the internet and social media extends the lifespan of a story, compared to traditional forms of media. Chris Anderson devised the Long Tail theory in 2004 and published it in the magazine *Wired*, of which he is currently the editor-in-chief. He says:

> The theory of the Long Tail is that our culture and economy is increasingly shifting away from a focus on a relatively small number of 'hits' (mainstream products and markets) at the head of the demand curve and toward a huge number of niches in the tail. As the costs of production and distribution fall, especially online, there is now less need to lump products and consumers into one-size-fits-all containers. In an era without the constraints of physical shelf space and other bottlenecks of distribution, narrowly targeted goods and services can be as economically attractive as mainstream fare.

Anderson uses online music and video to further illustrate his point, explaining that songs not played on the radio on a daily basis and video not available on the television can be accessed via the internet at any time, even years later. This contrasts with traditional print media, which tend to be disposed of within 24 hours of reading. He argues that 'social media management will quickly grow into a big deal for all organizations' and that 'the days of worrying about only your own website ended in 2007'. Online coverage can be recovered from the bottom of search engine rankings with a bit of effort and some intervention and inclusion of hyperlinks and generating of relevant online discussion.

HR Media Ltd, like most modern media and PR agencies, recognises the importance of social media. Martin Webb, senior account executive at HR Media Ltd, says:

> Our job is to raise and protect the profile of our clients. We would have used traditional media to do this previously. However, social media allow us to reach an even bigger, more varied and ultimately more immediate audience. It would be ludicrous to ignore this... The media have changed dramatically in the last five years. In ten years' time, not only will the media have changed even more dramatically – but so will the people who use it. The generation which engage with social media are getting to the point where they are becoming the influencers, the buyers, the advisers, the sellers – so public relations needs to follow suit if this is where public relations is happening!...When we discuss social media with our clients, we are always very keen to stress the importance of a solid website. Social media can perform (if done properly) a very cyclical purpose, in that they can reinforce a message, or allow the user to reinforce the message, but ultimately if someone is reading that message and wants to find out more, the central web presence is the final destination. It can be frustrating if a company is active and visible in social media, but invisible (or poor) as an end product (from our client's perspective).

Every day, clients ask practitioners like Martin, 'How do I set up Facebook groups?', 'Is it worth setting up a Twitter account?', 'What do you think of a YouTube channel?' Martin judges the platform on its merit, the purpose of the coverage and the audience the client is trying to reach before engaging. The biggest danger is to set up a social media platform paying lip-service to the latest fad and not keep it going. That is far more damaging than any negative comment on a social media platform.

Example

Increasingly, PR agencies are offering a web-video service that can be uploaded to YouTube, the second most used search engine in the world. HR Media won a video competition for WhizzGo cars. The video was used on WhizzGo cars' website, Twitter, blogs and Facebook pages. Anyone searching for WhizzGo would find lots of ways into its services via the web and vice versa; the services would find them.

Challenges in the workplace

While you may think you're controlling the reputation of your organisation on the internet via your corporate website, a range of different, sometimes conflicting, messages may be being made public by employees, as well as customers and other external stakeholders. Comments about employers have appeared on sites like Facebook and Bebo, many with very positive outcomes, but where a company's reputation is brought into disrepute by a disgruntled employee, you may be faced with a challenging situation: how to deal with negative comments appearing publicly, and how to deal with the employee.

A set of expectations is commonly being implemented into employee guides to advise employees of the consequences of misusing the internet in work time, as well as posting negative messages about employers. Some of the negative comments could be a case of whistle-blowing, where a company claims to operate in a certain way and the employee feels compelled to dispel any misrepresentation, especially if these concerns have been ignored through formal internal channels. So the message is to always 'practise what you preach'. Don't claim on your website to be highly ethical if, for example, your recycling policy is weak or you suspect that your suppliers are bypassing rules on child labour.

As discussed, some blogs may appear above your company website in search engine listings. The key message is that organisations are no longer able to control the messages or discussions about them and they need to engage with online debate or disgruntled employees to overcome any challenges. The answer may be as small as making improvements to communication internally so all staff are fully aware of the company's objectives, or at the other end of the spectrum it may mean making fundamental changes in the way you do business.

Example

In January 2009 an environmental group challenged Starbucks to stop running cold water taps constantly during opening hours, at points where staff would rinse utensils. This request went unheeded by Starbucks until it was brought to the attention of journalists via a series of blogs. The story became a top national news item and Starbucks was forced to agree that it would stop such practices and revise its policy in order to save water. This story conflicts with Starbucks' website, which claims that the environment is at the heart of its corporate responsibility agenda.

It is very difficult to stop information leaking out, but guidance to employees and transparency in your business practices is essential to minimise any risk of negative comments on the internet. Don't be panicked if you find your company is being discussed online; it may not always be bad. You must engage in debate and overcome negative perceptions through positive consultation and demonstration of business practices.

Using the internet to gain a competitive advantage

The internet is truly remarkable, and essential for commercial success. It has changed the way businesses operate. Online information is dominated by content developed by those external to the organisation. Online users are inquisitive and questioning, with an increasingly high proportion of purchases now being made online, and information provided online affecting purchasing decisions. The PR profession, as well as search marketing agencies, are very aware of the opportunities and are working hard to convince clients that while print coverage is still very important, it is being dwarfed by the relevance of online communication, owing to its reach and opportunities to engage with stakeholders.

Example: Best job in the world – you can't have failed to miss it!
In January 2009, Queensland Tourism promoted the Barrier Reef islands via a job add for 'the best job in the world' as an island caretaker. Although a real job opportunity, it was designed to attract interest and visitors to the region. It became one of the most successful viral campaigns, winning the Cannes Lion Award and attracting nearly 10 million visitors to the tourism website, 34,684 applicants from 201 countries, and more than $100 million worth of media coverage (advertising-equivalent free publicity) from a budget of $1.2 million.

To protect information excessively can be a big turn-off for stakeholders, and pose questions like 'What have they got to hide?' It also shows a lack of expertise and understanding of the increasingly transparent external environment. Companies that have embraced the internet now compete on online exposure and are judged by their transparency and online engagement.

> Life can only be understood backwards, but it must be lived forwards.'
>
> Søren Kirkegaard, 1967

Hence, the future is unknowable yet recognisable, and the outcome of everyday online interactions among people, entities and environments will increasingly provide your greatest opportunities for customer satisfaction and corresponding competitive advantage.

Summary and activities

Key points

- **The internet has revolutionised the way that companies are able to communicate with stakeholders, and the newspaper industry was one of the first industries to react to the potential of the social media.**
- **Companies are engaging with stakeholders via blogs and social networking sites, such as Facebook, LinkedIn and Twitter, and developing interactive websites to gain feedback and engage in discussions that may influence their brands.**
- **Managing your reputation online is essential in protecting your brand and business. Reputations painstakingly built over years can be destroyed in a few minutes by disgruntled bloggers, negative comments and poor results on either comparison or social networking sites.**

Questions

1. Why are companies moving on from static websites?
2. Why does the online coverage of your business last longer than printed coverage?

Activities

- Visit Chris Anderson's site to read more on the Long Tail (http://www.thelongtail.com/about.html).

- Set up a social media microsite like Twitter and see how many people you get to follow you by discussing developments in your sector. Can you become an online industry expert?

Stakeholders and customers: how to develop and maximise relations

Have you ever stopped to consider why you are working in the manner that you are? Why are you attending particular meetings? What have you gained from the interactions you've had with colleagues? What have you learned that's new? How have the meetings moved things forward (if at all?) How do your internal relationships compare with those that are external?

A useful tip is to keep a diary (or critical incident log, if you prefer!) of how meetings have helped you to achieve your company's objectives. After a few months, reflect on your entries and ask yourself some questions. Are you attending because:

- **it's voluntary or obligatory?**
- **because of the apathy of others?**
- **it's routine or a crazy impulse?**

You'll find that your drivers are complex, vary with time, change depending on circumstances and are completely different from those of your colleagues. Having a better grasp of your own drivers, you'll be better placed to understand how stakeholders react to your communications, and will be able to provide useful information and resources to facilitate their decision-making.

Naturally, there's more to communications than simply serving up broadcasts for colleagues to consume. Indeed, the delivery of successful corporate communications depends upon the interactions between providers and consumers. You may have colleagues who are already producing PR and corporate communications with clients. These colleagues can also make major contributions towards establishing internal customer satisfaction. Every communication represents an opportunity to show your company in a positive (or negative) light. Understanding internal customers' needs and having their best interest at heart sends a powerful signal. That said, not all stakeholders are equal (Figure 6.1), hence you need to be aware of the impact your communications could have.

Obviously, care is needed when communicating with internal stakeholders. While not all stakeholders are equal, they all have the capacity to create issues that will need effective PR solutions.

		Level of Interest	
		Low	High
Power	Low	Shareholders	
	High	Staff	Managers

Figure 6.1 Stakeholder power matrix

PR as an internal marketing tool

Many companies claim that their people are their most important 'asset', which begs the question – do they treat their staff as such? Internal marketing (see Figure 2.2, page 17) is a well-established concept but is often poorly practised. Effective internal marketing needs senior management commitment, which sadly is not always provided. You may need to sell the benefits of change to your colleagues or get them to see the big picture if customer service expectations are to be exceeded and not just met. PR is the obvious tool to help promote internal marketing, assuming you recognise the need to satisfy colleagues as well as clients. Many departments carry out internal marketing on a regular basis. Consider the role of IT; there really is more to it than 'Have you switched it off and on yet?' Modern IT departments increasingly talk about satisfying customers.

So, we need to know how internal customers react when they're 'buying' our communications and what influences these processes. Remember, you may be communicating with colleagues in other departments of your company or within the same parent organisation.

Internal marketing as an ongoing communications process

Communication is an ongoing process with no clinical start and end. As the world changes, so do our stakeholders and publics, hence our communications need to adapt and evolve to move with the times. This can only be achieved by entering into regular, honest dialogue with your internal customers (Figure 6.2).

Every time you receive stakeholder feedback, your organisation has grown stronger. This also applies to other stakeholders in business environments in which you operate.

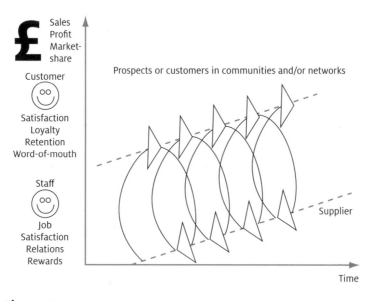

Figure 6.2 Benefits of a healthy dialogue

Macro- and micro-environments

Wherever and whenever you see changes in your business environments (Figure 3.2, page 28), you must change and adapt, otherwise you risk being left behind and could suffer quite serious consequences. Being a consumer yourself, you will appreciate that we often value goods (or services) that appeal both socially and psychologically. Often, consumer issues are highly charged with emotion as well as clear thinking. Consumers attach varying degrees of symbolism and values to their purchases. Increasing numbers of consumers pay premium prices to buy products, say those identified as Fairtrade, that match their value systems.

The risks of not understanding such issues are twofold: first, if your product offer doesn't align with consumers' values, then increased customer losses are likely; and second, consumers these days not only 'vote with their feet' but contribute to the plethora of social media sites. As discussed previously, you need to consider how you can use PR to influence them in the right direction – that is, your company.

The decision-making process

No one is saying that price is not an issue for consumers, but it is rarely *the* issue in decision-making. Historically, campaigns sought to encourage customers to buy a product or service – that is, close the deal. In doing so, marketers too often simply listed the product's features without relating how they helped solve customers' problems. Pre-Web 2.0 this may have been enough to satisfy customers, but these days online consumers expect much more than just the traditional transaction; they expect service, reliability, website personalisation, easy use and fun. Yes, instead of the traditional notions of purchasing, customers are seeking information on benefits while enjoying themselves in the process. Indeed, the thrill of the auction is a key element of eBay's business model.

However, the advent of Web 2.0 user-generated communications tools, such as social networking sites, has shifted the emphasis (from the supplier simply closing the deal) to helping consumers to make decisions prior to the purchasing decision itself. Answer this: are you now engaged in trying to sell what you think they want? Or is it a case of finding out what information consumers need to make better decisions?

If you're simply focused on closing the deal, you could be in trouble. Figure 6.3 shows the traditional business-to-consumer (B2C) decision-making process. The transition between each stage could be affected by feedback from social networking sites, blogs and other user-generated tools. Bear in mind that the time dedicated to the various stages differs, depending on whether the purchase is:

- **A routine or repeat purchase of something bought many times before, such as bread, milk or other fast-moving consumer goods (FMCG) items. This is a quick process with low risk and hence little monitoring of the decision.**

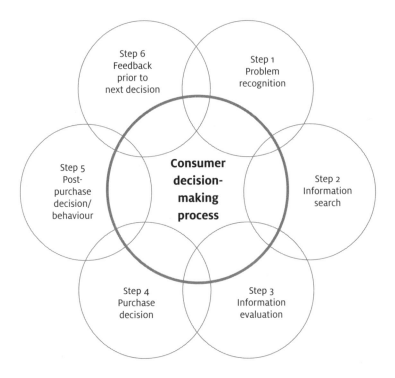

Figure 6.3 Consumer decision-making process

- A purchase with medium or limited risk, where the item is bought infrequently with a higher degree of risk, say an annual holiday or a flat-screen television for home use.
- A rare, high (or extended) risk where if it goes wrong the implications may be long-term – for example, buying a house, a wedding dress, a new high-value car, etc.

Simply put, every stage of the decision-making process presents opportunities for prospects or customers to seek opinions or input from a blog, forum, social networking site and/or price comparison site. Wherever possible, your company can use PR to provide the information needed to help customers make the right decision – that is, buy your goods and services!

The decision-making unit

Traditional marketing has always advocated awareness of the decision-making unit (DMU) (see Figure 6.4).

The DMU is a simple model that implies passivity – that is, all the actors simply sit there, not interacting with each other. Experience tells us, however, that the DMU stakeholders can impact each other greatly, in some cases energising each other, in others providing constraints. In small to medium-sized enterprises (SMEs), different stakeholders can form part of multiple scenarios, for example as initiator and user but not buyer. With the advent of Web 2.0 the concept of the DMU still

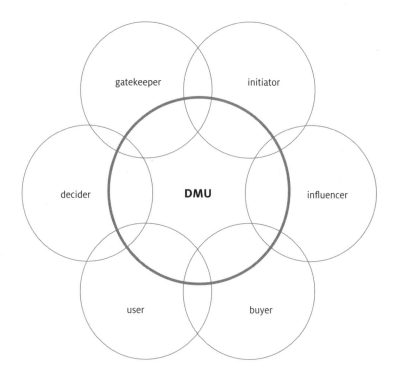

Figure 6.4 Decision-making unit (DMU)

applies. However, different stakeholders not only fulfil differing roles but often contribute to online debates via a forum (or indeed multiple forums), blogs, social networking sites or comparison websites. A further complication is that these stakeholders may also use multiple media channels simultaneously. Such people are known as media multi-taskers.

SMEs

Marketing within SMEs is different from that in larger companies. SMEs tend to adopt the characteristics of their owners or managers and tend to be more intuitive. This lends itself well to social media sites such as LinkedIn. SMEs are economically of increasing importance. In the United Kingdom there are 2.5 million enterprises, of which 99 per cent are SMEs. However, marketing texts have largely ignored SMEs, as they predominantly focus on larger companies. This trend is now changing, with increasing numbers of SMEs buying and selling goods and services online. The business-to-business (B2B) decision-making process (Figure 6.5) applies to both SMEs and larger organisations.

Some barriers to adoption of e-commerce by SMEs do exist, such as the following:

- **SMEs lack awareness of sources of assistance, such as grants.**
- **They perceive IT skills problems.**
- **They feel their company is of too small a size to benefit.**
- **They perceive the required technology to be too expensive or too complicated or incompatible with in-house systems.**

Try to anticipate these issues when communicating with SMEs. It is not always easy to find information on the latest social media tools, as was proved during a discussion at the Academy of Marketing conference. A room full of distinguished marketing academics (who among them have written hundreds of different

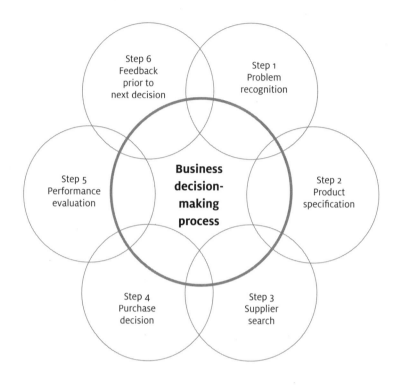

Figure 6.5 Business decision-making process

titles) expressed concerns regarding discussing the latest Web 2.0 tools, such as Twitter, in their texts. They felt that things move so fast that by the time their texts are published, the tool might have become passé. This attitude is too product oriented when what is needed is a more customer-centric approach. The tools are indeed changing, but a constant is that customers need to know the benefits of what you offer them. That never changes!

Customer satisfaction

As exchanges bring suppliers and customers together, relationships are formed, and you need to develop the initial relationship by finding out as much as you can about the client's needs. Put simply, if you give customers what they want, they'll return to buy your goods and/or services. Servicing existing customers is much cheaper than attracting new ones, therefore customer satisfaction enhances sales turnover and profitability as well as increasing your market share. Satisfied customers tend not only to be repeat buyers but also to tell their friends, families and colleagues. Conversely, if they have a poor experience, they tend to tell even more people about it! Think 3:10. Everything good your company does will lead to customers telling three people about their experience, whereas for everything bad it's 10!

You probably now better understand the need to move away from single transactions and towards effective management of long-term customer relationships.

Emotional intelligence

How many times have you sent an e-mail and as soon as you've hit the 'send' button you've regretted it? How often has someone misinterpreted the tone of an e-mail? Or has your humour been misconstrued? As a manager, you may have explained difficult decisions to your staff and still they've not reacted the way you'd anticipated. Well, you're not alone, and many, often highly intelligent, people suffer the same malaise. Communication is not simply an intellectual exercise, it's social and emotional.

Increasingly, consultants are referring to emotional intelligence (EI) as complementing the traditional IQ form of intelligence. When communicating with your stakeholders and publics, you essentially need to devise an engaging message that will have a positive impact on the audience – that is, increase interest, desire and action among the target audience. EI helps with identifying, understanding, integrating and managing emotions – both one's own and those of others.

EI is highly useful in teamwork, particularly in complex multidisciplinary scenarios. The EI of a team is not merely the sum of individuals' EI. Rather, EI is generated within the team as norms are created, mutual trust develops and a group identity is formed – qualities that promote cooperation and collaboration. In short, EI provides understanding of how the emotions experienced by individuals affect the work of the team. EI is 'more than just a passing fad... [it has] captured the long-term interest of employers and educators' (Grewal and Salovey, 2005: 339).

Summary and activities

Key points

- In order for you to be successful in your communication strategies, it's crucial that you listen to what stakeholders are saying and actively encourage their participation in the process. That said, not all stakeholders are equal.
- Customers should be at the heart of all business decisions and activities. However, organisations should be both inward and externally focused to truly understand and react to changing trends.
- Anticipating your customers' needs is a start to developing a relationship with them. Providing them with what they require by satisfying their needs will entice them to come back time and time again. Over time, customer needs change and your communications activities need to change with them.

Questions

1. Why do some consumers take a long time moving through the consumer buying process?
2. What are the key factors that influence a consumer's buying behaviour?
3. How does purchasing differ between a consumer and a business?

Activities

- Map the different needs and motivations of different 'actors' in your DMU? What are the key benefits that your organisation can attain by recognising the different roles within the DMU?

- Reflect on the impact of social media sites on your decision-making process (DMP). How does your company tailor its communications to address DMP variations among your customers? Do you know what your key customers want now? In 18 months? Or in 3 years? If not, why not?

- Think about your behaviour. How have your needs changed as you've grown older? Can you think of any organisations that satisfy your needs really well in a way that encourages you to go back time and time again? Likewise, can you think of any organisations that have disappointed you? If you have been disappointed, how would you advise them to improve? How have you reported your disappointment to your networks and communities?

For the more academically inclined, the following article on SMEs is useful:

Gilmore, A, Carson, D and Grant, K (2001) SME marketing in practice, *Marketing Intelligence and Planning*, 19 (1), pp 6–11

For light reading (?) on SMEs, look at the following:

EC (2005) [accessed 25 August 2009] European Commission Recommendation 2005/361/EC [Online] http://europa.eu.int/ISPO/ecommerce/sme/definition.html.

Crisis, what crisis?

Often, managers are judged on how they deal with both unexpected and expected issues that arise. Crisis management is big business for many PR agencies, which build reputations on helping businesses out of sticky situations. This chapter considers some of the measures that may save you from having to bring in the agency experts, with the added associated costs.

Planning

You can plan for dealing with a crisis. Many organisations devote huge resources to simulating crises in order to understand how they might deal with the real thing should it happen. If a damaging scenario may arise, then it's far better to anticipate it than to ignore it. The risk may seem insignificant. However, you must ask yourself what the outcome might be should it arise.

While you could try to plan for all identifiable eventualities (eg fire, flood, contract breaches, financial mismanagement, flaky customer services, flagrant abuse of staff, etc), it's more realistic to consider crisis as a risk element that can either be anticipated or take you completely by surprise. PR can help you through a crisis or assess elements of risk by understanding what the implications might be, for both your internal and your external audiences. It can be used to support strategic planning as well as implementing tactics to minimise the risk of a crisis.

Who to communicate with during a crisis

Your stakeholder mapping analysis (Chapter 6) will shift dramatically during a crisis. Dormant or latent stakeholders may become very active during a crisis. Consideration must be given to their perspectives and possible activities; will they support you in a conflict, and your efforts to minimise risk during your damage limitation activities?

Communicate with key stakeholders proactively before they read about your organisation in the media or on social media sites. You must know how to engage them in order to win their support. The danger of ignoring some stakeholder groups is that doing so could result in the period of crisis being extended, or the crisis escalating and becoming even more difficult to manage.

Saying sorry... *mea culpa*

Too many organisations deny any wrongdoing during a crisis or are too slow to admit responsibility. This leads to further scrutiny and criticism, and a protracted period of crisis. Stopping, or killing, the story may be crucial to managing the situation. This might not mean saying sorry as an admission of guilt, but simply apologising for the inconvenience caused, while you investigate further. The media and other audiences will be more sympathetic to your situation and be more inclined to work with (rather than against) you to come to a speedy conclusion of the situation, especially if you're sincere!

Demonstrating your sincerity may require further evidence that you're addressing the situation and investigating bad and good practice. This should include a thorough investigation of any wrongdoings. This doesn't mean going on a witch-hunt to find someone to blame, but responsibly addressing the situation and monitoring the public mood towards your organisation.

Being proactive as well as reactive

Keeping the communications lines open may mean opening up your organisation to further investigation. Responding to media enquiries in a professional, timely manner is essential, as is considering ways of rebuilding confidence in your brand or organisation. Many organisations experienced in dealing with crises understand the value of being proactive as well as reactive in the face of adversity.

Example

In July 2005, following the London suicide bombings in which 56 people died and over 700 were injured, Leeds Metropolitan University (LMU) had to respond to intense media interest as journalists tried to uncover information about the bombers. As the police investigation to find the bombers led them to communities in and around Leeds, the world's media followed.

The media, equipped with only the bombers' names, scoured the region for clues to where and when they may have met. This put immense pressure on LMU as rumours spread that the bombers had studied at the university. With the police still to release the identity of the bombers, the university would have breached Data Protection Act 1998 if it had confirmed the names as those of students, current or past.

This gave LMU's communications team much-needed time to work with local stakeholders to establish as many facts as possible, including scouring its own database to establish whether the names being quoted in the media matched any on file. Meanwhile, the country was in shock as details of the devastation caused by the bombers were made available, as well as the tragic stories behind those who had lost their lives.

LMU proactively contacted Leeds City Council as well as other higher and further education institutions to establish whether they were under the same pressure and whether there was anything they could do to support each other. From this consultation, LMU established that a large number of local residents were being made temporarily homeless while the police investigation was under way. LMU's communications team arranged for members of the displaced communities to stay in the university's halls of residence.

By the time the police confirmed the bombers' identities, LMU was able to announce its contribution to the displaced communities, at the same time as confirming that at least one of the bombers had studied there. The news release and subsequent press articles led with news of the displaced communities being accommodated in the university's halls of residence. News that a bomber had been a student was barely mentioned in the press. Despite being drawn into the crisis unexpectedly, LMU took control of the situation. It established a crisis team early on with the following key objectives:

- Manage the flow of information.
- Avoid distortion.
- Actively promote positive stories but be sympathetic to the mood of the nation as the country was in shock following the horrific bombings in London.

- Identify and communicate with priority stakeholders.
- Operate on a business as usual basis.

The communications team brought in colleagues from other departments to help manage the huge number of media calls. It created teams to monitor developments in the press, to communicate proactively with stakeholders and to continue with ongoing projects.

LMU's communications team had established protocols for dealing with the media, which included regularly reminding colleagues not to respond to media enquiries directly but to refer journalists to the communications team, who had good working relations with the regional media. This enabled them to work with the media in a number of areas, including finding out what themes of the crisis the media were concentrating on, to establish how LMU could contribute proactively as well as reactively.

This example clearly demonstrates the need:

- **to develop a crisis team who can be objective, not dealing with front-line queries from journalists;**
- **for good relations with the media during calmer times, which can help during a crisis;**
- **to know your key stakeholders during a crisis;**
- **to understand where and when it's appropriate to be proactive;**
- **for sensitivities around issuing positive news stories in crises;**
- **to use legislation, for example that on data protection, to give you much-needed time, even if it's only a few hours;**
- **to take control during a crisis, if possible.**

Never say 'no comment'

Saying 'no comment' when questioned on a situation can give the impression of being guilty. It infuriates the media and the public when organisations respond in this way, and it can make a bad situation worse. Companies that refuse to engage with the media and the public will encourage them to seek other sources for the information they need. Journalists are especially sophisticated at using contacts and tools to get the answers they require, often at the expense of those who refuse to engage in discussion with them. Other sources include the internet, the emergency services, industry experts, local MPs and councillors, employees current and past, neighbours, customers and clients.

Talking to the media during a crisis

You must quickly establish your key objectives, which initially may focus on damage limitation. Whatever your objectives, it is important to communicate clearly, concisely and confidently, and to maintain control of the situation. It is not always necessary to put a spokesperson forward to face the media. If you're worried that he or she might not be able to deal with a barrage of questions from an aggressive media, simply issue statements via e-mail or your website.

During a crisis, large numbers of journalists want answers, hence it is often more effective to issue a holding statement, simply stating that you're investigating the situation and will issue more details shortly. This will buy you time and reduce the need for you to organise press conferences or provide opportunities for journalists to come to your premises during the crisis. Such visits are inadvisable as they can add an unwanted element of stress to a tense situation. Issuing regular statements via e-mail or your website can help to feed the media's insatiable appetite for news without letting them take control of the situation.

Journalists are trained to persist with their enquiries and can put people on the spot with questions they won't or can't answer. Statements reduce the opportunity for further questions to be fired at individual representatives.

Example

When a London to Glasgow Virgin train was derailed near Carlisle in February 2007, Virgin boss Richard Branson was on the scene within hours of the accident, talking to the press, empathising with the passengers and generally being a great ambassador for the Virgin brand. He praised the train driver, Iain Black, for his bravery in supporting his passengers at the crash scene. Branson knows exactly how the press works and how to manage a crisis situation sensitively and sympathetically. His approach generally lessens negative speculation and poor publicity.

Crisis manuals and simulation

Many practitioners refer to crisis manuals as 'king' in managing a crisis effectively and many produce lengthy documents full of great ideas and action points, which in reality are rarely used during a crisis, owing to their static nature. An effective crisis manual will contain details on communications systems to implement when needed, including basic messages, identifying key stakeholders or audiences, up-to-date contact details and protocols. It should be easy to use and provide clarity in often confusing times.

Conducting a crisis simulation is a useful exercise that can create the atmosphere of a crisis in a controlled environment. It should also highlight gaps in procedures and provide the opportunity for staff to understand the important roles they would play in a crisis. Repeating the simulation at regular intervals will make sure that any weaknesses are identified. A simulation may involve inviting external parties, including the media and the emergency services, to take part. This will ensure that all key parties recognise the role they play and all key players can be acknowledged as crucial to the process.

Summary and activities

Key points

- **A bad situation can become a crisis if not recognised immediately. Crises can be sudden (the cobra effect) or slow-burning, rumbling on (the python effect). How you deal with the situation will depend on how long the crisis lasts.**
- **Organisations need to take control of matters as quickly as possible. Developing a crisis team to respond to the situation and develop proactive as well as reactive responses is crucial. Identifying quickly the roles people will play in dealing with the crisis, from the receptionist to the MD or CEO, will ensure that resources are used effectively.**

Questions

1. What are the crucial elements of dealing with a crisis?
2. Who should address the media during a crisis, and in what way?
3. What role can staff play during a crisis?

Activities

1. **Consider how well prepared your organisation is for dealing with a crisis.**

2. Review your crisis procedures and simulate a crisis situation on a regular basis.

3. Think of the current crises that are facing businesses and organisations – you just have to read the news to see examples of good and bad crisis management.

Internal communications

Employees must be viewed as ambassadors for your business and should have a real stake in making your business a success. Keeping them well informed and engaging in two-way communication, which allows for them to feed back their constructive views on the business, will enhance the relationship and add value to your business.

As well as being essential for large employers, where two-way communication between staff and management is deployed at a global as well as a local level, internal communications is beneficial for small companies to share information and allow staff to feed back ideas and issues that will help the business to perform better. It is also essential for companies that want to rebrand, so that management have a clear understanding of how stakeholders view the business, with internal stakeholders being a very important group.

Traditionally based in human resources (HR) or personnel, internal communications has developed into a thriving discipline in its own right. It has grown in size and stature as management recognise the important role that staff play in the success of an organisation.

Key strategic areas that internal communications can affect include:

- **supporting major change;**
- **communicating messages from the management;**
- **communicating the business's mission or vision or values;**
- **raising awareness of business issues and priorities;**
- **increasing and maintaining the credibility of the management;**
- **motivating employees;**
- **allowing feedback from staff;**
- **improving the communications skills of management.**

Example

Tesco recognises the value of its employees, stating that they are as important as customers with regard to the success of the business. It regularly asks staff what is important to them, and responds accordingly, treating them with respect, providing managers who help them, and creating interesting jobs and opportunities for progression. In return, Tesco's staff are fully aware of the company's objectives through its 'Every little helps' strategy. Tesco understands that if staff have rewarding jobs, they're more likely to go that extra mile to help customers.

Controlling the message

Internal communications is the discipline that engages with staff through a series of tactics, including notice boards, meetings, intranets, events and newsletters. It is important that you listen to staff and let them know that you acknowledge and value their opinions and, where appropriate, act on them.

In order to communicate with staff effectively it is important to understand the business's overall strategy so that you can share with staff your vision and how they can help you to achieve it. Too many employees work in silos, concerned only with their area of expertise or discipline, and lack awareness of, and even interest in, how the wider business functions. However, with a bit of effort from management to help them understand how their role contributes to the 'bigger picture', staff will take pride in their work, which in turn benefits the organisation.

Schemes such as profit sharing, comments boxes, share options, as well as pension contributions from employers and holiday allowances that go beyond statutory provisions of employment law all add to the well-being and satisfaction of employees. Conditions in the workplace that go beyond health and safety legislation and ISO 2001 also help to make employees feel valued. As employers, you will be judged by benchmarks set by law, as well as by other employers. Generous employers understand the value of respecting their employees and providing a 'better than satisfactory' working environment.

Getting to know your employees

Too many employers have assumptions about how to make employees feel valued, often based on their own experience rather than on research. To really get the best out of your staff, you must invest time and effort in getting to know them and in understanding their needs. The most effective way to gain an understanding of and empathy with staff is to conduct an audit.

The audit

Find out what your employees understand about your business and identify gaps in their knowledge, and issues with their moral engagement and motivation. You can conduct an audit via a number of routes:

- Focus groups, although they are best conducted anonymously by a person impartial to the business.
- Questionnaires. Keeping them brief and offering an incentive to complete them usually maximises the quality of data being returned. They can be conducted via online surveys or on paper, with employees being given a deadline to complete them.
- Team meetings conducted by line managers as part of a team-building exercise or scheduled update meeting.

Evaluating an audit

You must demonstrate a commitment to the process of gathering information to understand your staff's perceptions of the business and issues affecting their job satisfaction. If staff don't feel they're being taken seriously, then you must address this by making more of an effort to listen to them. As Tom Peters famously said, manage by wandering around: walk the floor, shadow the workforce, spend one day a month in their workplace doing their jobs to appreciate their perspective more effectively. The knowledge you gather will identify patterns and inconsistencies that you can act upon in a positive way.

Frequency of staff auditing

Best practice would recommend an annual formal audit with regular discussion going on throughout the year. Audits should always be voluntary, to ensure staff provide honest and considered responses. To maximise participation, you must act quickly on recommendations and comments by staff. Report the highlights of the audit as well as any negative issues raised. Consistent criticism must be addressed to reach a positive outcome in order to keep morale high throughout the year.

Remind staff of the impact the previous audit had on the company and how their input led to positive changes. There are standard audit questionnaires you can use or adapt for your business, most offering a selection of qualitative and quantitative questions. Survey Monkey offers a free online questionnaire service for questionnaires of up to 10 questions, with a great tool for analysing results quickly. Examples of questions in a standard questionnaire are shown in Table 8.1.

Table 8.1 Sample questionnaire for a staff audit

	Strongly Agree	Agree	Somewhat Agree	Somewhat Disagree	Disagree	Strongly Disagree
I know what's expected of me and my job						
I have clear information about how I do my job						
I feel comfortable with what I'm asked to do in meeting my job expectations						
My supervisor and I have a clear understanding of what I'm expected to do and how I'm to carry it out						
Management do a good job communicating their decisions to everyone						
Management allow me to execute my work responsibilities with little or no supervision						
I understand the company's priorities						
I feel I'm given opportunities to contribute to the direction of the department						
I'm given opportunities to comment on the company's direction						

What if you don't like the feedback?

Even during a strong economic climate in which the job market is buoyant, it's equally important to maximise engagement with employees to minimise the costs of recruitment and employee turnover as the choice and competition from employers increases. The messages may differ depending on the economic climate. However, a truthful and open approach is always essential. As previously discussed, people are the most important asset in your organisation and it's vital to retain their talent as long as possible.

Whatever the outcome, you must address it personally and professionally. It's no good ignoring issues, as they're unlikely to go away without your input. Addressing the issues raised may be an uncomfortable experience, but once they have been dealt with, everyone should feel more valued and respected. If you engage with staff and reward them for their efforts, you will reap the benefits of having a committed and focused workforce, on message and on your side. So, don't hide in the office. Get out there and meet the teams that help you to make your business what it is.

Example

A survey published in June 2009, conducted by the financial communications agency FD, polled 524 white-collar workers and found worryingly high levels of employee dissatisfaction as bosses dealt with the tough recessionary times. A minority of employees (44 per cent) felt that their CEO showed strong leadership, and only 28 per cent trusted messages from their CEO more than 'a little'. Businesses expect people to work harder, often for less money, during a recession, and this is a tough act to balance for any boss. The focus on employee engagement is never more important than during difficult times.

FD's survey found that 33 per cent of employees will look for another job if the boss fails to address concerns and 67 per cent do not have common face-to-face contact with bosses. Eighty-one per cent said face-to-face contact with their line manager was the most trusted form of communication.

Resources for internal communications

Large companies have dedicated internal communications specialists who will constantly audit, evaluate and communicate with staff on behalf of the senior management. Internal communications is a growing specialism that has developed alongside the need for organisations to communicate strategically with all their external stakeholders. Internal communications practitioners will also ensure that senior management are fully engaged in communicating with staff via events, meetings and, increasingly, video casts and audio casts broadcast on the company intranet or in-house TV screens.

Tactics for internal communications

Company newsletter or magazine

An internal communicator's role usually involves producing and editing newsletters, both online and paper copies. Companies may release a weekly, fortnightly, monthly or even quarterly publication to staff, made up of regular news items, and a notice from the boss. Regular items might include articles on staff achievements, both professional and personal, outstanding performance in the workplace, and a regular item from the senior manager on business matters. Newsletters should be colourful and easy to read, with lots of photos to break up the text and illustrate the articles.

Intranet

Establishing an intranet involves developing a web-based forum for communication with staff, and is restricted to access by staff. Staff must make an effort to view this sort of medium, and it should not be relied on as the sole way to communicate with staff.

Events and meetings

Most staff would rather see managers face to face than only see their faces in newsletters and on websites. A combination of formal and informal opportunities for staff and management to meet should be staged throughout the year. The content of the events will depend on their degree of formality, but such events should not be underestimated as regards their role in developing great employee relations.

Notice boards

A much more traditional way to communicate with staff, notice boards are still very effective, especially for organisations that have staff who do not regularly sit at the same desk or have access to the internet. Very often the content is used to signpost staff to other sources of information, as the level of detail you can post on a notice board is usually fairly minimal.

The water cooler effect

Informal channels of communication, such as employees gathering around the water cooler, photocopier, corridors and post room, are where the latest gossip tends to be shared. Rather than frowning on these 'natural' phenomena, employers should recognise them as useful opportunities for staff to feel engaged, and as adding satisfaction to their jobs. These informal channels can be used to communicate messages, often more quickly and effectively than the formal channels.

Staff use of the internet

Most companies will have a website and encourage staff to read notices from management via it. Increasingly, companies are developing their own social networking sites for staff. These are aimed at reducing the amount of time staff who use computers spend on 'non-work-related social networking sites', and they have a role in gathering feedback and the latest trends from staff.

While there have been incidences of staff abusing the internet at work, even posting offensive comments about employers, many employers are recognising that this can be due to poor internal communications, employee dissatisfaction, and a lack of transparency and clear protocols by employers. It is perfectly acceptable for employers to discipline staff for such activities, but they should question why staff feel the need to 'go public' with their views. Often it is a lack of good two-way internal communications that leads to this situation.

Employee communication needs

The basic requirements for good internal communications are built around the needs of employees. As a guide, these needs include:

- general information about the organisation;
- specific information about their role in the organisation;
- clarity around their role;
- a clear understanding of the organisation's vision;
- information on workplace practices;
- opportunities to be involved and consulted;
- feedback on performance;
- access to training and development;
- access to communication channels.

An internal communications strategy that addresses these needs effectively should produce an engaged workforce who enjoy their work because they feel valued.

Organisational culture

It is widely accepted that organisations need good leaders to provide a clear direction for the success of the business. This success includes recognising the need to engage with staff at all levels of the business. Good leaders define the culture of the organisation, and the very survival of the business depends on their commitment. The leader's ability to communicate effectively is important to the credibility and quality of internal communications.

David Thomas, from Harvard Business School, stresses the importance of multimodality in communication, saying:

What you say is only the beginning... Your behaviour, your actions, and your decisions are also ways of communicating, and leaders have to learn how to create a consistent message through all of these. It's been said many times, but leaders lead by example... Communication can't always follow the top-down model... With the fluidity of information in business today, leaders need to be masterful listeners; they need to be able to receive as well as send. Individuals at all levels of an organization need to be able to take responsibility for their decisions. They've got to feel they have a sphere of influence that allows them to have their own version of enacting the organization's vision and strategy.

Rosabeth Moss Kanter, also from Harvard Business School, puts it another way: 'Leaders must wake people out of inertia. They must get people excited about something they've never seen before, something that does not yet exist.'

There needs to be an alignment of the interests of the organisation and the interests of the individuals. Incentives must be meaningful, whether they are monetary or intrinsic.

Ethical employers

Employees are just as keen to work for an organisation they believe in as they are to earn money. Graduate surveys consistently reveal that the type of company they work for is more important than salary for most. So make sure you appeal to the best and can make them as committed to the business as you are, so that you retain them for as long as possible.

Don't fall into the trap of feeling that a job is 'just a job' for your employees. The psychological contract between employer and employee is complex and multi-layered. As employers streamline activities, contracting services and products from abroad, jobs are rarely considered secure. With a much higher turnover of staff than ever before, companies must acknowledge the complex relationship with staff.

The new 'psychological contract' with staff is based on offers of training and development, to keep staff employable not just by their current employer but for the future, as well as fair pay and treatment in return for employee commitment.

We'll discuss ethics more in Chapter 11.

Summary and activities

Key points

- Staff should be one the greatest assets of an organisation. They must be treated well and engaged with to ensure they contribute to the success of the business.
- Conducting annual audits on employees' understanding of the business's aims and objectives will allow management to understand what is important to staff and to implement change where appropriate to improve employer–employee relations.
- Many tools are available to ensure you communicate effectively with staff. Using a combination of tactics that will allow management to communicate with all staff and allow them to feel valued will reap rewards in terms of employee engagement, which in turn benefits the organisation.

Questions

1. Why do companies engage with internal communications?
2. How important is internal communications to the overall PR/ marcomms efforts of an organisation?
3. What sorts of tools are available to use to communicate well with staff?

Activities

- Consider the tools that you have found most effective during your career in allowing your employer to communicate the key values and strengths of the business to you.

- Put yourself in the position of employees across your organisation, at a range of levels of seniority and ask yourself what would make them feel more engaged. Are they already fully engaged and do they understand the key objectives of not just their department but the wider organisation?

- Have a look at surveys like the *Sunday Times* 100 Best Companies to Work For (http://business.timesonline. co.uk/tol/business/career_and_jobs/best_100_ companies/). What sort of internal communications do they use?

Getting the facts right: using research to create a competitive edge

As discussed previously, before you can satisfy customers and add value to their experience, an understanding is needed about who they are, what they require and what influences them. The way we acquire this information is through marketing research.

> Fortune favours the prepared mind.
>
> Louis Pasteur, 1854

Pasteur's observation seems obvious, and yet business history is littered with examples of ill-prepared communications campaigns for product launches or repositioning efforts failing owing to a lack of research. Carrying out good-quality research is undoubtedly the best way to prepare for any communications strategies that your company will undertake.

Consider the number of decisions you make on a daily basis. Some decisions may be fairly minor; others may be important, with far-reaching consequences. Good-quality information helps to reduce risk and create more certainty when making decisions. You'll be well aware that there are often a variety of answers or solutions when making decisions. Marketing communications research can provide information to support you when making decisions within a given set of circumstances or parameters.

Types of research

The term 'marketing research' is very broad and encompasses many different 'types' of research which you may be able to use, so let's consider some alternatives.

Market research

Market research is research specifically undertaken on the market type (ranging from monopoly through duopoly and oligopoly to the theoretical perfect market), barriers to entry, market size and market condition. This type of research is particularly useful when your objectives are geared towards entering new markets and you have to design a communications campaign that is fit for purpose. You can use a number of frameworks to provide a structure. For example, Porter's 'five forces' model looks at aspects such as the competitive intensity, new entrants, the power of buyers, the risk of substitutes and the role of suppliers. This type of research can really focus in upon the key features of the actual market in which you operate.

Product research

Under the heading 'product research' you'll seek information specifically on the product, the product's features or the desirability of the product. As previously discussed, you can use PR to improve your feedback from social media sites. This approach is often used in new product development where you're seeking consumer insights and perceptions of the actual and potential product(s). It can also be used if you start to encounter any problems with your products. As discussed in Chapter 2, when a company is moving from maturity to the decline stage (Figure 2.4, page 19), you can use PR to identify means of extending the maturity stage research by engaging users in feedback exercises on social media sites. Remember, all audits are inherently political, as they can involve parties having to be self-critical. To overcome the bias (of a supplier asking for comments on its own products), you can use a third party such as your local business school or PR consultants.

Distribution research

Distribution research is a key area for your company as you must identify where the consumers and/or customers think your products ought to be sold. During the development of your entire marketing communications strategy, decisions regarding how to support the distribution of your products are key. Again, this could be a central piece of your communications research: How do you use your distribution network in order to maximise your competitive advantage? How do you use PR to communicate benefits to retailers who may stock competitors' products alongside your own? To an extent, manufacturers lose control of the communications process when their goods enter the retail space and you can use PR to maintain contact with the end-user and the retailer. In the 1970s a major retailer would stock, say, 5,000 product lines. Now it will carry 50,000 lines and you can use PR to differentiate your goods once the research has indicated the possibilities.

Research methods

Research by its very nature is often systematic and scientific. Don't let this put you off! You don't have to collect the data yourself; your PR practitioner, consultant or agency will gladly liaise with a marketing research agency to do it on your behalf. You still need to fully understand the benefits that the research process offers and how it works. Why? Because once the data are presented to you, it'll be your decisions that will lead to implementing changes in your company.

Generally speaking, all research should follow a logical approach (Figure 9.1).

Let's consider in more detail what is involved in conducting research.

First, it is important to define the research question. Just why are you conducting this research? You will be trying to solve a particular problem or answer a particular question, for example 'Why are the sales of this specific product falling?'

Be as specific as you can about the question you wish to answer. This is important as it provides focus for the whole

Figure 9.1 The systematic marketing research process

research project. You can't afford to be too broad with your question as this could create a research project that's too woolly to produce meaningful answers. But nor do you want the research question to be too tightly focused, as this could constrain the research and you may miss unplanned opportunities. It's not easy!

Once you've identified the research problem, you then need to set your research objectives. As in Table 3.1 (page 32), objectives should be SMART.

> **Example**
> Research problem: To increase brand awareness of Leeds Business School by more than 3 per cent during 2010.

Create the research plan

As in Figure 3.1 (page 28), research is better if it's planned. You'll need to think about the different types of data that you'll need, resource demands, access and so on. Let's consider the type of data required. There are two types: secondary and primary.

Secondary data

Generally speaking, most researchers tend to collect secondary data before primary data. This is because secondary data are data that already exist. Such data can come from internal sources such as company reports or previous market research reports. External sources such as government publications, newspapers, magazines and directories are also useful. The internet enables secondary research to a greater extent than ever before, although its scale is problematic, given recent (already out-of-date) estimates of 65 billion pages in the web. Large research agencies, such as Mintel and Nielsen, also publish research reports which you could purchase or commission. However, they can be costly.

Secondary data are not specific to your research question, nor will they be up to date or particularly accurate, which are the key disadvantages. However, they may give you a starting point, or a feel, for the optimum direction. Although there are these disadvantages, the reason we often use and start with secondary data is because doing so is cost-effective (the data already exist), you do not need to be a skilled researcher to collect or use them and they are relatively quick to collect. Therefore, if you work as a sole trader or in a small organisation, the use of secondary data to try to find the solution to your problem is realistically the starting point for you.

However, using secondary data will get you only so far. As the data are not specific to helping you answer your research problem or question, and because they may be out of date, and therefore slightly inaccurate, the chances are that you will need to collect more up-to-date and relevant data. The data you collect for the first time, which are commissioned to be specifically focused upon solving your research problem and objectives, are known as 'primary data'.

Primary data

Primary data are based upon specifically answering your research problem and objectives. Therefore, they are specific, relevant, timely and, if collected and analysed properly, accurate.

There are different ways you can collect primary data. One of the factors that plays a part in deciding which technique you use to collect the data is whether you wish the research to be structured using quantitative data or qualitative data. These two terms sound intimidating but in fact they are very simple and straightforward.

Quantitative data

Quantitative data are data based upon numbers that are representative of a larger population. Care has to be taken as it's easy to generate superficial figures that suggest trends that may not be there. That said, well-designed 'quant' research, based on either secondary or primary data, can provide useful information on consumer trends.

Example

When psephologists Ipsos MORI carry out research to predict the result of UK general elections, they often use quantitative data that seek to represent the whole voting population. They typically poll a sample of 1,500–2,000 prospective voters and generate results that are accurate to plus or minus 3 per cent. When it's a close-run thing, 3 per cent may not be accurate enough and they would need a much larger sample. Alternatively, they could triangulate their findings with those of other surveys.

Questionnaires

Ipsos MORI would use a questionnaire as the method to collect raw data. You would then analyse the data to deduce information, in this case the public's voting intention. Raw data are not the same as information.

Questionnaires can be administered in a number of ways:

- **face to face, with the questionnaire being completed by either yourself or the respondent;**
- **by telephone;**
- **by post;**
- **by e-mail;**
- **online, via a pop-up.**

Each of these techniques has strengths and weaknesses. You need to acknowledge these to avoid bias, which is the bane of good research. Consider posing the following question to male respondents:

Have you used, or would you use, a condom?   Yes/No

You can be fairly confident that the answer is honest and lacks respondent bias. You could ask this using any of the above methods.

The follow-up question is:

What size?

As you can imagine, this poses a number of questions that need to be addressed to avoid bias. You must consider the sensitivities of the researcher *and* the respondent. Hence, this question would probably be better asked in a non-face-to-face way, such as by e-mail or by phone.

Respondent bias can also result from over-long questionnaires. Table 8.1 (page 101) is typical of a questionnaire that uses a Likert scale (that is, with responses ranging from 'strongly disagree' to 'strongly agree') in an attempt to avoid the shallow nature of some quantitative research. The example provided is fine, but try to avoid pages of questions.

Questionnaires are very useful if you need to collect data from a large number of people. A key issue to consider is that if you're looking for trends in a large body of people, you will not have the resources to question them all. Hence, you'll need to question a representative sample of your target audience. It's a balancing act, as the more people you question in your target audience, the greater the degree of accuracy your results will have.

Questionnaires do provide you with the opportunity to also ask open-ended questions to collect qualitative data. An example is 'What is your opinion on banning smoking in public places?' However, if you're using lots of these in your questionnaire, then you probably should have used a qualitative research design in the first place.

Qualitative data

If you are wishing to collect data that are based upon people's attitudes, opinions, feelings or perceptions, then a qualitative approach is required. Often, how we feel is a greater force than how we think cognitively. Any long-standing football fan knows that the heart rules the head, particularly for supporters of the majority of teams that rarely win trophies! Qualitative research is often used to ascertain consumers' feelings regarding new products or services.

However, the choice is governed by your research problem and objectives. You then have to undertake the collection of primary data, which is quite a skilled task with a variety of methods or techniques. The two most common methods used to collect qualitative primary data involve the use of focus groups and interviews.

Focus groups

To set up a focus group, you select 6–12 respondents from your target audience and ask them questions. Focus groups are very useful when you're developing new products or services, as you create the opportunity to interact with a selection of your target market and perhaps show them a prototype of the product. What do they think about its design? Size? Colour? Weight? Name? How much would they pay for it? Where would they buy it? A lot of useful qualitative data can be collected.

Interviews

An in-depth interview is just with one respondent. Therefore, the interviewer can really probe for in-depth answers, feelings, opinions, etc. However, the technique can be costly, as it is time-consuming and done on a one-to-one basis – but the results are both timely and, hopefully, accurate.

Choosing the most appropriate method to use can be difficult. The trick is to really understand what it is you're trying to find out – hence the reason you need to understand your research question and objectives very well and also understand which methods are useful for collecting which type of data. You also need to consider your limitations and circumstances. It's also important to understand whether instead of using qualitative or quantitative data, you may actually need a blend of both, which in reality is often the most suitable.

Analysing and presenting the findings

Once you have collected the data, you then have to analyse them. What do they all mean? How can your company use the data? This can take time and skill, hence many PR consultants use specialist research agencies to plan their research and collect, interpret and analyse the data.

Quantitative data are easier to analyse as they are well suited to statistical analysis, spreadsheets or simple graphs. Packages such as SPSS exist to facilitate complex analysis of large amounts of data. Qualitative data must still be analysed to identify themes and trends. Simply offering a few respondent quotes is not usually enough.

Once the analysis is complete, your PR representative will want to coordinate the presentation of the findings to the appropriate stakeholders. This may include your manager, director, customers – not just yourself! Rest assured that good knowledge gained from well-designed research can only strengthen your company's position, so don't be surprised if others may find the results and conclusions interesting as well. Hence, you should put some effort into making the report stand out.

A common mistake is that researchers and marketers make the report easy for themselves, not the reader. Have a beginning, middle and end, with a logical flow from start to finish. Don't start discussing things in the conclusions section for the first time!

Marketing research is at the heart of most marketing decisions. To remain competitive, innovative and attractive to the customer, we must constantly evolve our products, services and organisations. Marketing research is central to providing us with the data and information to help us to do this successfully. It goes without saying that the research should be conducted in an ethical fashion. If in doubt, refer to the Market Research Society's code of conduct.

Summary and activities

Key points

- Marketing research is used to provide up-to-date, accurate information to help companies solve problems and lower the risk in important decision-making.
- Marketing research is systematic in nature and a basic process is to be followed.
- Secondary data are data that already exist. Such data are cheap to collect and readily available, and a non-skilled marketer can collect and use them. However, they are often dated, therefore inaccurate and not specific enough.
- Primary data are data that a marketer collects for the first time. They are therefore specific, timely and accurate. However, they can be time-consuming and expensive to collect. A degree of skill is also required to collect and analyse the data accurately.
- There are a variety of techniques available to collect primary data including questionnaires, focus groups and interviews.

Questions

1. Why do marketers need to invest in marketing research?
2. What are the risks associated with marketing research?
3. Why is the setting or research objectives so crucial?

Activities

Look at the material in your office: past research projects, sales statistics, competitor information, pricing initiatives – they could all be regarded as secondary data and could be useful to refer to in the future. So, create a simple information system in your office. Ensure that you file these documents (don't throw them away!). Even if you don't find them useful initially, somebody else might!

For an excellent introduction to social and market research, have a look at the following textbook:

Adams, K and Brace, I (2006) *An Introduction to Market and Social Research*, Kogan Page, London

Also look at a variety of websites. The Market Research Society's code of conduct is essential reading for those involved in marketing research (website: http://www. mrs.org.uk). Others to peruse are:

http:// www.mintel.com

http:// www.datamonitor

http:// www.marketing-intelligence.co.uk

10

How much should good public relations cost?

While today's new technologies offer exciting communications choices, there are also challenges. When marcomms work well, they can provide many benefits for the brand, the company and, more importantly, the customers. However, when they go wrong (and they go wrong with worrying regularity!), they can have devastating effects. Not only can precious time, money and resources be wasted, but your brand name, brand equity (the value of the brand) and the reputation could all be adversely affected. Because many of your comms activities will be in the public domain, your mistakes are there for all to see: your intended receivers, your competitors and (in some cases worst of all)... the media!

Which marketing strategies do you wish to drive with PR?

Marketing communications

You may wish to complement your traditional PR activities through generating buzz in other ways, such as guerrilla marketing or getting bloggers to write about your company. We need to acknowledge this and remember it when we are creating, planning and executing our comms activities. When faced with making purchase decisions, consumers often seek information to support their decisions, particularly when making larger, riskier purchases. They'll read magazines (eg sector-specific publications or consumer-friendly titles such as *Which?*), use the internet to glean more information (from social networking sites, public forums, comparison sites, opinion leader sites and blogs) and, above all else, turn to the people around them for advice and guidance. They'll ask colleagues, friends and, most of all, family. It's a common practice for a consumer to access all of the aforementioned sophisticated communication materials and still heed the advice and opinions of those closest to them more than the supposed 'experts'.

Positioning

Positioning is simply about how your customers (and prospects) perceive your company in relation to the competition. Hence, you need to consider how good their communications are. As a matter of course and practice, you should always be monitoring your competitive environment (see Chapter 2). What communication tools do your customers use? How often? Are they successful?

Product portfolio

Are you centring your messages on a product or service? If so, what points do you need to exemplify? After considering the above factors, you also need to think about the customers in more detail and then select the most appropriate strategy to reach them with your message.

How much to invest in PR?

The answers will very much depend on your situation and how you interact with your marketing environments (see Figure 3.2, page 29). Let's assume that you're looking for a PR agency to handle a new product launch. You approach four agencies and their quoted 'budgets' range from £10,000 to £200,000. How do you evaluate their plans?

The cost of hiring a PR agency varies greatly, depending on how established the agency is and the level of service that you require. Large companies can pay hundreds of thousands of pounds on generating PR, an amount of money that would put many SMEs out of business. Many PR firms will also act as a media centre, taking enquiries from journalists, and may offer a guarantee of some kind, which can reduce the risk of spending thousands of pounds for no end product. So it really depends on:

- **What marcomms tactics are you using already and how are they working?**
- **How much do you need to do?**
- **How much can you afford to do?**
- **What is your marketing budget overall and how much of it are you willing to devote to PR?**

Consider the budget allocation decision you'll have to make; PR may take 5 per cent of your budget or it may be 100 per cent. It depends! So take a look at your overall marketing budget, your target audience and your goals. While it's true that you usually get what you pay for, should you automatically discount the lowest budget (or the highest, for that matter)? Remember, you're looking for your PR to be efficient *and* effective.

So we now need to reflect on the key question: How much are you going to spend? This is a key determinant of your communication choices. Indeed, whether strictly correct or not, the decision is largely driven by your budget, which in turn impacts on whether the choices of communication tools open to you will widen or, conversely, become extremely narrow.

What is your budget?

First of all, asking how much a PR campaign should cost is a lot like asking how much an advertising campaign or a sales promotion campaign costs. An ad campaign can cost £5,000 or it can cost £250,000,000. Likewise, PR is a tool that can be used by all organisations and hence can benefit them in different ways. So how much your organisation needs to do is a question that has to be judged on its own merits. A PR campaign can range from:

- being free: many PR practitioners carry out *pro bono* work for charities or causes with which they're sympathetic;
- very low cost: at Leeds Business School we're always looking for clients who are willing to offer internships (eg a day a week or in blocks of weeks), placements or work experience for PR undergraduates; companies new to PR may seek an initial 'one-off' project to test the water;
- medium cost: use of a dedicated consultant with high-sector experience; retaining a small to medium-sized agency with limited resources; ad hoc use of a larger agency when fit for purpose;
- higher costs from large, possibly multinational agencies that will take on all of your communications efforts with truly global reach.

Naturally, these different approaches will have a range of costs (Table 10.1).

Ad hoc PR, like ad hoc marketing in general, is to be avoided as it's a lottery more than it's social science. Once you've worked with an agency or consultant, you'll be satisfied that PR is effective and you may want to commit to hiring a PR agency on an ongoing basis. For this the agency will put together a couple of press releases each month, and develop a longer-term PR strategy. The cost for this typically starts at £1,000 per month.

Table 10.1 Costs of PR

Company Type	Daily Rates	Budgets
Independent PR practitioner/ consultant	£75–£150 daily	Up to £5,000 for monthly retainers
Independent PR practitioner/ consultant (10 years' experience)	£150–£300 daily	£3,000–£10,000 for monthly retainers
Small PR firms (5–25 employees)		Up to £5,000– 10,000 per month
Large PR firms: junior representative		£7,000–£25,000 per month
Large PR firms: senior partner		£20,000–£100,000 per month minimum up to £1 million

Time is money

Remember that even if your company isn't investing time in generating material, your agency or consultant will be! Pascal has often been quoted as writing 'I'm sorry for writing such a long letter but I didn't have time to write a short one.' Experience shows us that writing a 200-word piece of PR copy can be as taxing as 'knocking off' 1,000 words. Certainly CIPR and CIM professional students recognise the challenge of writing to a word limit. Typically, a 1,500-word case study or feature article may require 20 hours of the creative department's time; this involves researching and polishing off after numerous revisions. As discussed in Chapter 4, press releases are the building blocks of PR programmes, and two-page releases may easily require 5–10 hours to write and distribute to the appropriate outlets.

Even the smallest PR programmes should budget 20 hours per month for basic media relations. Larger companies often budget hundreds of hours per month! A guide is to map all of the publications you (or even better, those that your customers) deem to be useful and allocate a proportional time for media relations activities. Hence, if your company needs regular exposure through, say, 20 key reporters, reviewers and analysts, consider budgeting approximately 20 hours per month.

Remember that there are many incidental 'out-of-pocket' expenses (for postage, photography, long-distance phone charges, couriers, etc) to be factored in. These could range widely, from £100 to £2,000 per month. Distribution costs, assuming the release will be mailed to, say, 50 media outlets, should not exceed £250. On a one-off basis, some companies will simply put together a press release, send it out and hope that it delivers results. This costs in the region of £200–£400 and is low cost but risky in that results are far from guaranteed. To keeping mailing costs as low as possible, companies have increasingly moved towards e-newsletters.

Example

EFL is a leading UK-based supplier of hubs and routers to ISPs. It e-mails a monthly newsletter to 5,000 prospects and customers at a cost of £75. The content is designed in-house, so naturally the company has some HTML experience. Its scheduled PR programme is highly effective as its staff strive to keep the material therein of high quality. There is always a demand for news of benefits and means of adding value, particularly if featuring testimonials where products or services have helped a company solve a key business issue.

Large PR firms can charge anything from £1,000 to £5,000 for a single press release. However, for this they'll drill down into your company (hence understanding your aims and objectives) and sector before creating and distributing a press release. Large PR agencies will want to follow up their efforts as a matter of professional etiquette.

As Table 10.1 illustrates, £3,000 a month will retain a good PR company. However, you must ensure you're getting value for money, and set aside a number of days or hours for the effort needed to do so. You need to be confident that the agency or consultant you engage has access to the media contacts that relate to your company. PR is like every other walk of life (and business) in that people buy from people, and PR consultants generally have only limited outlets where they have excellent relationships and can get you coverage. Beyond their sphere of influence they may struggle to provide the reach and access your company needs.

Many clients believe that it is imperative to understand exactly what PR is delivering to their bottom line, arguing that PR agencies (and staff) need to comprehend the financial aims and objectives of the company as well as barriers to achieving competitive advantage.

You'll certainly want to know whether your clients perceive your media presence favourably over a period of time. If they don't, ask them what is needed to improve their perceptions. If any of their suggestions are adopted, use this as a powerful tool. Clients simply love to know that their advice has been taken on board. Is your agency providing the right coverage, frequency of release or improved positioning in the media? Try to come up with measurable parameters for evaluating the effectiveness of your PR from the clients' perspectives. Bear in mind the following:

- **Favourability of coverage is not the same as volume of coverage.**
- **Advertising value equivalents (see page 132) and Opportunities to See (see page 136) are not easy to measure.**
- **Qualitative information is often more useful than quantitative measurement.**
- **Measurement of changes to your company or brand reputation may happen over a long timescale.**

- **It's not simply how many times your company is mentioned; rather, it's about how your customers' (and prospects') views and behaviours have changed.**

If you try to skimp on publicity efforts by budgeting only a couple of hundred pounds per month, don't expect the world. The publicist will be able to spend only a few hours working on your account, so don't expect to be on television and in the best newspapers around. The old adage is true: you get what you pay for!

The do-it-yourself option

There are plenty of examples of people who are not PR professionals but practise PR as a matter of course to ensure their business or organisation maintains and develops a healthy profile and reputation. Bill Gates, Richard Branson and, more recently, Barack Obama are just a few of the high-profile people who understand the power of PR. Never ones to say 'no comment' or turn away from a difficult situation, they have earned respect based on transparency and a willingness to engage with the public.

As an ambassador for your organisation, you and everyone who represents your business, because they are employed by you, buy your products or use your services, have the ability to influence the reputation of your organisation. It is important therefore that you harness PR opportunities, recognise who your brand ambassadors are and build and maintain excellent relations with all parties involved. You can do this informally as well as formally but you must always do it in the knowledge that whatever you and your ambassadors do and say about your organisation may impact on its reputation and success.

You may look to hire a PR agency on a one-off or an ongoing basis. PR should be a continuous process but you may be happy with generating some initial media coverage but subsequently managing your PR activities in-house. Doing your own PR costs you nothing but your time, although you'd be wise to do a lot of reading on the topic before you start, speak to your local business school, study a CIPR-approved course or even pay for a few hours of coaching from a PR professional.

There is a news medium where you can circulate press releases yourself: PR Newswire (www.prnewswire.co.uk). It offers a range of services and targeted release mechanisms. It is a bit 'scattergun' but does work. Last time one of us used it, the cost was about £250 to go to thousands of news desks.

Make sure the chemistry is right

Entering a new relationship with a PR firm should be a very positive experience for both parties. Good PR agencies and consultants will be willing to work with you to establish a realistic budget at the beginning of the relationship. The odds are very good that the two companies will work well together, almost seamlessly. When business partners respect and trust each other, everyone benefits. Isn't that what building a relationship is all about? It is important to take care of your PR team. These are the people who will tirelessly promote your company and seek ways to improve your competitive advantage.

Evaluation

Whenever you seek to communicate benefits to customers, whether it's a piece of PR, a sales promotion, an ad or a direct mail letter, you must always be able to measure its effectiveness and decide whether the communication has worked and achieved its objectives. You can easily spend large amounts of time and money on your communication activities, so you need to know whether they're working. If they are... great! But why have you got it so right? What can be taken from this success to create another? Conversely, if the communication is failing... why? Is the message unclear? Is it the media chosen to carry the message to the receiver? Is it down to noise? Is the encoding incorrect? With potentially high costs involved, you must be able to rectify mistakes quickly and learn so that future communications will hit their intended marks.

The process of evaluation can be quite simple, especially if you have set SMART objectives for your PR activities (see Chapter 3). SMART objectives might include changing legislation or ensuring that a set number of delegates attend an event. But they could be as subtle as changing people's views and attitudes. Whatever your objective, it is essential that you identify from an early stage how and what you are going to evaluate to measure the success of your PR activities.

Building evaluation into your programme of activities from the outset ensures good accountability and effective management. In practice, evaluating campaigns and PR activities can be fraught with challenges and disagreements. PR is a discipline in which experienced practitioners regularly debate the value of various types of evaluation, and purchasers of their services may challenge the benchmarks drawn up for purposes of evaluation.

The CIPR has produced guidelines and toolkits on evaluation but there is no defining common standard. PR is subtler and more difficult to quantify than other communication disciplines, such as direct mail or advertising, and the evaluation methods, while varied, are essential. They are often dynamic and flexible to enable change where required and reflection at all stages of implementation.

Evaluation of media coverage

Still the most common form of PR activity, media coverage can be evaluated in a number of ways to create some meaningful understanding of the success of your coverage.

The crudest, yet still the most commonly used, is to compare the size of a piece of coverage gained with how much it would have cost to place an advert in the same media outlet. Advertising value equivalents (AVEs) are used by PRs to demonstrate to clients and business that PR is more cost-effective than advertising and a more credible way to get your message across to readers or viewers.

A quarter-page advert in your trade publication or regional newspaper might cost £1,000. If you gain a quarter-page article, whether through an interview with a journalist, via your news release or self-generated by a journalist, you might compare the value of the coverage gained with what you've saved in terms of advertising.

Example 1
In 2008, Ultragen wanted to launch an anti-ageing skincare device called Stop, at a high price and with no confirmed retailers on board.

Objectives:
Launch the product and build awareness of the technology behind it.
Secure credible retail partners.

Tactics:
With research, the PR team gathered endorsements from credible medical and cosmetic professionals. Trial products were offered to beauty bloggers. The supermodel Marie Helvin was secured as the 'face' of Stop and a photocall was staged in the window of Selfridges. Local press events were held around the country, receiving regional coverage, and product samples were sent to celebrities.

Evaluation:
A total of 116 articles appeared in titles such as *The Sunday Times Style*, *Grazia*, *She*, *Harper's*, *Tatler* and the *Mail on Sunday* as well as regional media. GMTV's *LK Today* programme gave a product demonstration.

Result:
Both Selfridges and Harvey Nichols were secured as distributors, along with smaller retailers. Harvey Nichols

reported that Stop was flying off the shelves, and placed emergency repeat orders in the run-up to Christmas 2008.

From this example we can see that Ultragen knew the market it wanted to launch its product at, it knew which publications would help it to do this, and it recognised that gaining endorsements from credible sources, using an appropriate celebrity, would maximise the results. Evaluation was ongoing, as monitoring the media was essential to keeping the story alive. The PRs would have been contacting relevant, targeted journalists as the coverage grew, using the hype around the product to create more coverage, as beauty journalists don't want to miss out on the latest technology.

Example 2
In January 2009, ancestry.co.uk acquired the rights to publish the London Metropolitan Archives, a collection of records detailing more than 400 years of London history.

Objectives:
To raise awareness of the online launch of the London Metropolitan Archives.
To drive visitors to the website www.ancestry.co.uk.
To boost subscriptions.

Strategy and tactics:
Research by the PR team worked out that more than half of Britons could trace a relative within the collection. They pulled out key facts concerning celebrities, and TV historian and actor Tony Robinson launched an event at the Guildhall

Crypts with a launch news release going to more than 200 national journalists.

Evaluation:
More than 30 journalists attended the launch event, leading to 108 pieces of media coverage, including 25 broadcast items and 40 websites that covered the story.

Results:
The Campaign led to a 30 per cent increase in traffic to the site and a 57 per cent increase in new membership over the two weeks following the launch.

Getting to the detail

This rather crude way of measuring the success of your media relations or news release is still considered to be very effective for most campaigns. However, it does not take into account whether the media coverage you gained was good or bad.

We know that on average only one in seven articles in a national newspaper is a positive news story. It would therefore be foolish to assume that all the coverage about us or our company is always going to be positive.

Key questions by which to test your media coverage will depend on the objectives but might include the following examples:

- **Has the article reached the most appropriate audience? It's no good celebrating coverage of your new service or product if the newspaper or magazine it has featured in is not read by your target audience.**
- **Have the key messages you wanted to convey been included? Does coverage of your new organic locally sourced product mention these key product characteristics?**

- **Has your brand name or company name been represented accurately?**
- **If you are launching a new website, does the article feature the address?**
- **If there are two named individuals included in the news release, are they each recognised, or are you going to have to explain to a key investor that they were not mentioned in your press coverage?**

In order to gauge media coverage most effectively, it is useful to develop a grid listing the key messages you want to communicate as well as assessing any negative comments and the overall tone of the message.

PR Week regularly conducts a survey to gauge which methods of evaluation PR practitioners have used. On average, 60 per cent use media content analysis or press cuttings to evaluate their activities. The next most popular technique is one called Opportunity to See (OTS), which is the number of occasions on which an audience has the potential to view a message.

Most 'cuttings agencies' – companies that scan the press looking for key words or names – include the circulation numbers of the relevant media. The circulation figure is usually three times the distribution figure. So if a newspaper sells 250,000 copies a day, its circulation figure is 750,000, as it is assumed that each copy is read by an average of three people.

Surveys and focus groups are also used to evaluation PR programmes. But it is generally accepted by practitioners that a range of tools and techniques is needed to properly assess PR impact.

Barriers to effective evaluation are also common, so avoid falling into the trap of not planning it into your programme of PR activity. Typical reasons for poor evaluation include lack of time, lack of personnel, lack of budget, cost of evaluation, doubts about its usefulness, lack of knowledge and exposure to criticism.

Summary and activities

Key points

- The cost of your PR will depend on the overall comms budget and campaign currently used. PR must be coordinated with your other marketing activities.
- The cost of hiring a PR agency varies greatly, depending on how established the agency is and the level of service that you require.
- Building evaluation into your programme of activities from the outset ensures good accountability and effective management.

Activities

- The Chartered Institute of Public Relations' website (http://www.cipr.co.uk) has useful sections. 'Looking for PR' includes definitions, a glossary and a guide to hiring a PR consultant, plus a PR directory.

- MediaUK is a forum for discussion and information for PR professionals in the United Kingdom plus an excellent media UK internet directory and a listing of the latest media news (website: http://www.mediauk.com).

- If you're interested in integrating PR into your marketing planning, buy Malcolm McDonald's book (*Malcolm McDonald on Marketing Planning: Understanding marketing plans and strategy*, Kogan Page, London, 2007). It hits the nail fairly and squarely on the head. For those teaching marketing planning it's an invaluable resource. Many of the lessons in general marketing planning apply to planning a comms campaign.

11

PR championing ethics and sustainability

When you are considering the challenges facing your company, a key question is 'Why would clients buy my products rather than those of a competitor?' Finding good answers to such thoughts is crucial. One answer is that consumption is social, in that when 'buying', we take on attitudes, beliefs, opinions and values from others, hence companies that are not aware of changes in society run the risk of alienating customers. This is the case with sustainability, which despite being missing from most marketing texts is increasingly important to key stakeholders.

The business of business is business...?

Sustainability is based on mutual benefit – that is, both parties benefit and can work together long term. Milton Friedman challenged the idea of mutual benefit, arguing that the business of business is business. That is, a company's only moral responsibility is to make money for its shareholders. He even argued that 'the social responsibility of business is to increase its profits', which somewhat dismissively alluded to the growing roles of social and societal marketing. Yet despite Friedman, more and more companies have espoused their green credentials while recognising how a widening range of societal issues, such as ethical practices, has gained importance with consumers.

It has been argued that Friedman's libertarian position leads to the establishing of non-sustainable structures, as was the case with the 2008–09 economic meltdown. Assuming Friedman's viewpoint to be one end of a sustainability continuum, its opposite can be deemed to be 'pure sustainability', which is philosophical, arguably spiritual and wholly dedicated to improving the human condition (Figure 11.1).

All companies are located on the continuum (knowingly or otherwise) and need to be aware of their position. Companies need to be able to position (or reposition) themselves within their markets in order to make effective decisions. If your research shows that your customers' perceptions (of your sustainability positioning) don't match your own, then you need to implement changes.

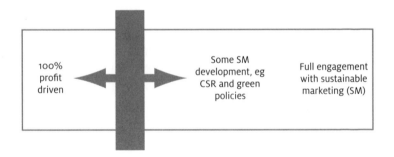

Figure 11.1 Sustainability continuum

Using PR to overcome barriers to sustainability

In the future, you'll probably need to operate in an increasingly sustainable fashion and you'll need to identify and remove barriers to adopting sustainability (Figure 11.2).

While it's unlikely that all of these apply to your company, you need to consider some of the following factors.

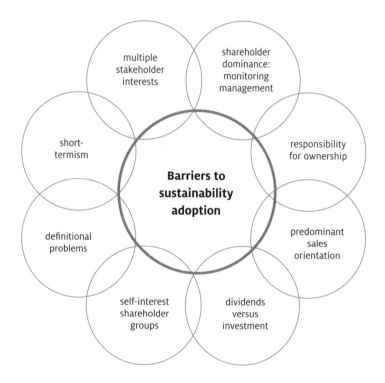

Figure 11.2 Barriers to the adoption of sustainability

Definitional problems

We live in fast-changing times and it's not surprising that many terms are used to represent new concepts. Even terms you'd think were well established, for example 'the environment', are used in myriad ways between differing texts and in some cases by the same author. It is prudent to consider such concerns since consumers often connect with broader environment issues. Their environmental interaction is important, intensely emotional and can affect their purchasing decisions.

It is therefore worth reflecting on key relatively recent developments that have shaped the sustainability agenda. The 1987 Brundtland Commission defined sustainability as 'development that meets the needs of the present without compromising the ability of future generations to meet their own needs'. In 1997 the issue was brought to much wider audiences (ie business academics and practitioners) when Hart coined the phrase 'sustainable development' in the *Harvard Business Review*. Soon afterwards, Elkington's 'triple bottom line' (TBL) appeared in the same publication. In the TBL the traditional economic focus (ie the company's bottom line) is complemented by the addition of new foci, namely social and economic responsibility. The Hart and Elkington texts are two of the most important recent contributions on the subject of business and sustainable development.

Since the concept of the TBL was coined, the sustainable business development concept has grown, often being referred to as 'People–Profit–Planet'. This may still be new to many practitioners (and academics!). However, elements of it have been practised for centuries. One often-cited example of sustainability in practice is the Co-operative movement, which has been practising a recognisable form of sustainable retailing since the 1840s.

One of the difficulties of defining sustainability derives from the multidisciplinary context. For example, town planners have a different take compared to marketers, who in turn differ from accountants. Even within disciplines there are many different definitions, with one study identifying over 500 attempts at developing quantitative indicators of sustainable development.

For a workable definition, consider the following:

> Sustainable Marketing (SM) involves principled marketing predicated on the tenets of the Triple Bottom Line. Hence marketing decisions should be ethical and guided by sustainable business practices which ultimately are the only way to resolve the tensions between consumers' wants and long term interests, companies' requirements, society's long run interests and the need for environmental balance.
>
> Richardson, 2008

This definition should act as a springboard for your company. Make sure that it is reflected in your mission and vision statements, and then use PR to ensure that all publics and stakeholders are aware of your position.

Shareholder dominance: monitoring management

Principals (ie shareholders and institutional investors) are aware that agents (ie directors and managers) may act out of self-interest and position the company in such a way as to reduce returns and share value. Hence, the principals incur the cost of monitoring the directors via annual audits, which are obligatory for all UK plcs. Too often, agents communicate with their shareholders only in the run-up to the AGM. This approach should be avoided and replaced by treating shareholders in the same way as you would customers. Use PR to build relationships, keep them informed, build loyalty and enhance shareholder satisfaction – and remember, loyalty is not the same as satisfaction!

Responsibility for ownership

One of the myths regarding business is that it's part of the problem, not the solution, and that issues such as sustainability should be the concern of politicians and governments rather than 'business'. On reflection, this approach is seen to be contradictory. 'Business' needs to be at the forefront of the 'sustainability' debate as trade largely takes place among companies, not governments. Also, it's not simply trading that is huge, but also the flow of capital in the form of foreign direct investment (FDI). In 2004, global trade ($7 trillion) was dwarfed by FDI ($17 trillion). Hence, 'business' has enormous potential to promote sustainable trade patterns. Also, 'business', rather than government, has the knowledge and skills to trade sustainably as well as helping to shape global sustainability guidelines and practices. If the Co-operative movement can thrive for 160 years, then other businesses can.

Example
Brownfield developments have found increasing favour among planners. However, retailers seeking development opportunities have complained about a lack of cooperation by local authorities, citing severe delays in winning planning approval. This macro-environmental interface is interdisciplinary in nature (being between the domains of retail marketing and the built environment). Retail developers may benefit from an improved PR role with the local community if it is their interest to gain advantage 'by favourably influencing the opinions of planners and the local community... [by] communicating the benefits of a proposed store to the relevant public' (McGoldrick, 2002: 267).

It is easy to see how sustainability 'ownership' can be fuzzy in some companies and hotly contested in others. Corporate social responsibility (CSR) is often controlled by human resource departments. Some organisations recognise the importance of CSR with elements in their mission statements (a strategic management decision), which may include 'green' issues (possibly a quality control issue), ethical supply policies (the purchasing department) and charitable links (all of the above!).

This corporate 'bun-fight' is reflected on the larger stage, where proponents of sustainable development differ widely in terms of emphases – for example, what to sustain or to develop, and when? In B2C sectors you could argue that responsibility lies with the service provider, the consumer, the community, the regulator or even the government. An example of governmental influence in the United Kingdom is the Companies Act 2006, which heavily affects CSR. Increasingly the environment will be used as a launch pad for governmental initiatives and legislation. PR can be an invaluable tool for informing the different parties and managing expectations.

Undoubtedly, when things are going well, everyone wants to stake their claim. However, when it goes wrong, where does responsibility lie? Recent studies have discussed corporate social irresponsibility, where CSR is abused by organisations seeking competitive advantage through misinformation. It is no wonder that we're increasingly sceptical of environmental claims, hence the rise of accusations of 'greenwashing'. Ultimately you must act in an ethical way and communicate transparently with your stakeholders.

Dividends versus investment

This question of whether to emphasise dividends or investment is more likely to apply to larger companies or those with active shareholders who seek maximum returns on their investment. As discussed, there are many tensions within companies, some of which are exacerbated by the (mis)use of the word 'sustainability' itself. For some, shareholder sustainability is the main corporate driver, featuring returning dividends and maximising share value for owners. Principals demand regular, stable dividend payments.

However, funds needed to pay dividends detract from the agents' ability to undertake new (sustainable) projects; principals want to sustain dividends to maintain market value. Shareholders' concerns (having funded the company through investment) should be acknowledged in conjunction with those of the stakeholders that enable the company to continue and thrive. Progressive managers should naturally cater for the lives and well-being of its micro-environmental stakeholders, such as employees, suppliers and the community in which the company is located. Hence, for most commentators shareholder sustainability does not equate to 'sustainability', and undoubtedly PR can serve a function regarding informing, and managing the expectations of, publics, including shareholders and institutional investors.

Self-interest shareholder groups

It may be stating the plain and obvious, but the terms used so far, namely 'business', 'company' and 'organisation', are somewhat nebulous. There are many differing types of multi-stakeholder businesses, including single proprietorships, partnerships, co-operatives, non-profit enterprises, social enterprises, private limited companies (ie those with 'Ltd' after their name) and public limited enterprises (plcs). Each of these categories differs in terms of aims, objectives, vision, culture, structure, and so on. In some companies, principals (aka shareholders) were deemed to be a key 'public' in that they had influence; however, they were largely deemed to be passive. Increasingly, shareholders are being referred to as key stakeholders in that they actively participate in the running of the AGM. Some principals acquire shares specifically to affect the running or direction of the company, which would usually be the domain of the agents (ie directors and managers). This may lead to strategic shift and/or drift, not to mention the potential for diminishing returns. Recently, shareholders have formed well-organised pressure groups in order to maximise their influence on corporate policy. These groups are often adept at using PR as a key tool in promoting their agenda.

Multiple stakeholder interests

Organisations do not exist in isolation, which renders Friedman's philosophy somewhat redundant. Simply put, companies affect the lives and well-being of their stakeholders and publics (Figures 3.2 and 6.1, pages 29 and 76). Managers have to interact with said stakeholders, such as employees, unions, suppliers, intermediaries, government and, most importantly, customers. Each of these may have their own agenda and/or be motivated by self-interest. In business schools we often preach the mantra of improving customer perceptions of added value. However, shareholder 'value' may come at the expense of customer 'value' and satisfaction. Companies could certainly use PR as a tool to address issues such as diminished job security, higher unemployment and poorer (perceived) products and services.

Short-termism

The economic difficulties of 2008–09 illustrated clearly that, for example, many financial institutions do not operate in a free market where they can do as they wish. Governments will always bail out financial institutions if the alternative is economically damaging. Cases such as Northern Rock should serve as an invaluable lesson in the danger of short-term approaches. In Northern Rock's case the business model was changed (after demutualisation) to an unsustainable model which strove for higher returns than had been the case in the company's long history as a mutual 'friendly' society.

In some cases, managers may wish to adopt policies beyond those demanded by legislation or regulatory bodies, such as being listed on the FTSE4GOOD index. This could incur costs that diminish market value or returns. Such action is often watered down if not prevented outright by fear of over-reaction by the short-termist markets. Hence, those with vested interests (such as institutional investors and free-marketeers) encourage managers to ignore investments in longer-run drivers of success such as sustainability. Many of these investors lost substantial funds in Northern Rock, which could have taken a different trajectory if they'd adopted a more sustainable approach... irony upon ironies!

Predominant sales orientation

A popular misconception is that PR promotes the (short-term?) selling of products to the target groups. Such sales orientations are now cited as contributing to consumers' increasing awareness of 'greenwashing'. Certainly Friedman's libertarian position contributes to the assumption that businesses advocate 'selling more', while 'sustainability' is about consuming less (Howell, 2006); therefore the two paradigms are diametrically opposed. Friedman's 'dominant' paradigm of free trade is increasingly criticised for being inherently unsustainable. However, economists still measure 'sustainability' by emphasising accounting approaches that focus on the maintenance of capital stocks and supply-side controls. Customers rarely feature in sustainability models discussed at the highest levels, such as the United Nations, the European Union or UNCTAD (the United Nations Conference on Trade and Development).

PR as an internal marketing tool

As previously discussed, internal marketing is a well-established concept (Figure 2.2, page 17) but is largely poorly practised. PR is the obvious tool to help promote internal marketing *and* the adoption of sustainable practices internally. After all, a key foundation of the TBL is 'people', and there are hundreds of studies that demonstrate the benefits of treating your people well. There has been a sea change in consumer opinion regarding the TBL and it is likely that marketing academics are trailing consumers, progressive organisations and other disciplines. Kotler now argues that marketer's lives will become more complicated. Meeting 'planet' costs may necessitate raising prices!

This does not automatically mean that the product will be harder to sell. However, you'll need to sell the benefits and add value. Also, you'll need to consider where your company should be on the 'sustainability continuum' (Figure 11.1). You may choose to commit heavily or to a lesser extent. One thing's for certain: in terms of sustainability there's no turning back.

Many managers have let operational effectiveness supplant strategy, particularly in scenarios where constant improvement is often seen as the route to superior profitability. Naturally, operations have to keep pace with customer change, and the move to sustainable marketing could be one such change. What is needed is not change for its own sake but the right change, and many examples exist of companies that have benefited by moving towards adopting TBL. What's needed is a framework for benchmarking (Figure 11.3).

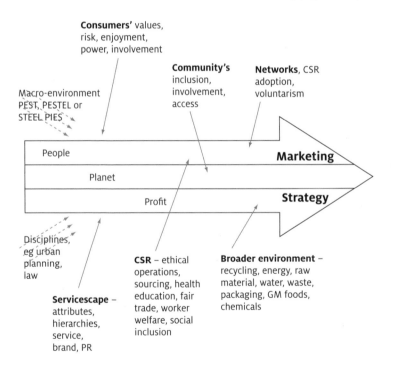

Figure 11.3 A framework for sustainable marketing

Managing change... or is it changing management?

Companies are made up of different systems that interact with each other and their respective environments. You won't be shocked by the notion that many managers protect their fiefdoms jealously and lack a vision of the bigger picture. A severe challenge for operations managers of 'non-enlightened' companies would be to operationalise the move towards sustainable marketing, as few models or theoretical constructs exist. It can be argued that too many companies are process or systems driven when they should be customer driven. Think about the term 'customer relationship management' (CRM). Surely this is a misnomer and we all should be seeking customer satisfaction management!

Anyway, you need to measure your effectiveness in all of the zones in Figure 11.4. There are already many tools out there. However, if you're struggling, you should contact your local business school, which will be more than happy to help you. Once you have your findings, plot them on a chart (Figure 11.4). Once you have done so, you can quickly ascertain the areas where you need to make strategic and/or operational changes. In the example provided you'd have to work on your communications with the networks and communities. Let's briefly consider how you might approach this challenge.

PR, networks and the community

Patterns exist in the adoption of CSR across differing organisations. Companies that are highly motivated may adopt an idealistic stance or even one of enlightened self-interest, whereas stakeholders on whom they rely may adopt CSR practices only when coerced. This potentially poses a risk for some companies. For example, Nike's poor PR resulting from allegations of child labour generated negative publicity that spread rapidly on social

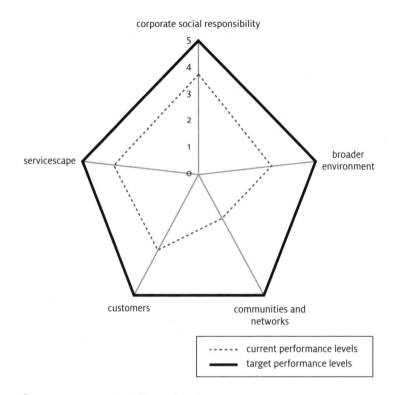

Figure 11.4 Sustainability polar diagram

networking sites. Reputations are easily tarnished by supply-side scandals concerning emotive issues such as child labour.

Hence, with your success depending on suppliers, it's important to ask yourself to what extent you can trust your supply network (a term preferred to 'chain') to act in ways you deem to be sustainable. Retailers, for example, are undoubtedly interdependent, networking organisations and will need to trust their partners. Trust can be shaped by previous experiences and cooperative efforts, and by the more general reputation firms build up. Sustainable marketers may also engender trust in like-minded consumers, and that trust can be grown, say through PR as a means of promoting positive word of mouth. Hence, it's logical to recognise the case for measuring trust within your network.

Developing trust within communities

Larger organisations often engage with the community only reluctantly. This attitude reduces the site of a new development to 'a plot' and something apart from the community. More progressive companies seek to establish relationships with local firms, consumers and regulators. Rather than simply complying with the minimum expectations, marketers need to be more inclusive and sensitive to stakeholders. You may easily benefit from improved PR with the community – not to mention enhancing your chances (as previously discussed) of success by favourably influencing the opinions of planners who receive positive feedback from the local community.

Example
Tesco's expansion into the United States with its Fresh & Easy chain has been based upon successfully engaging the host communities, often adopting a 'softly softly' approach that has contributed to its success. It describes the new chain as 'American stores for American people'. Even Tesco's UK tag line, 'Every little helps', is socially inclusive. Undoubtedly Tesco's success is underpinned by long-term research into the needs, wants and desires of its customers.

Using support mechanisms

Codes of conduct

You should use the wealth of good advice that is freely available simply by tapping into the codes of conduct of various bodies. They'll cover different aspects; for example, the Market Research Society provides a comprehensive code available from its website (www. mrs.org.uk). This covers any ethical research-based issues you may have. As we said in Chapter 1, the leading professional PR body is the CIPR. In signing up to its code of conduct, all members agree to:

- **maintain the highest standards of professional endeavour, integrity, confidentiality, financial propriety and personal conduct;**
- **deal honestly and fairly in business with employers, employees, clients, fellow professionals, other professions and the public;**
- **respect the customs, practices and codes of clients, employers, colleagues, fellow professionals and other professions in all countries where they practise;**
- **take all reasonable care to ensure employment best practice, including giving no cause for complaint of unfair discrimination on any grounds;**
- **work within the legal and regulatory frameworks affecting the practice of public relations in all countries where they practise;**
- **encourage professional training and development among members of the profession;**
- **respect and abide by this Code and related Notes of Guidance issued by the Institute of Public Relations and encourage others to do the same.**

Standards and guides

As well as codes of conduct, you'll find a range of 'standards' available to help you to measure your sustainability. For example, BS 8901:2007 provides a specification for a sustainable events management system. ISO 14001 is an internationally accepted standard that provides organisations with a planned set of criteria required for implementation of an effective environmental management system (EMS).

Also, you'll find that trade bodies and special interest groups have refined their own codes. As service industries make up approximately 85 per cent of the United Kingdom's GDP, it's fair to assume that some of the support materials for the event management sector will chime with other areas. Raj and Musgrave (2009) provide excellent coverage of event management and the sustainability challenge, and suggest the following support tools:

- **Sustainable Events Guide;**
- **SEXI: The Sustainable Exhibition Industry Project;**
- **The Hannover Principles: Design for Sustainability: Expo 2000;**
- **Staging Major Sporting Events: The Guide;**
- **The Sustainable Music Festival: A Strategic Guide;**
- **Green Tourism Business Scheme;**
- **The Eco-Management and Audit Scheme (EMAS).**

Frameworks to measure societal change

Governments, companies and charities use PR to promote campaigns that influence attitudes and behaviour towards issues such as health, tax rates, education and charitable giving. PR is valued by its success in altering societal views and behaviour. The ethical marketing, social PR and design agency Forster has developed Forster's Evaluation Framework to help clients recognise what is trackable and identify what they are prepared to track. The framework involves three stages:

1. *Audience Reach.* This measures where your message is being received, for example the number of hits in targeted media, search engine rankings, website hits, how many partners are involved in the coverage, attendees at an event. This can be measured via monitoring the progress of the campaign in a relatively simple way.
2. *Audience Engagement.* This involves asking questions of the 'reached' audience – for example how involved did they get, did they click through to your website, how long did they stay on your website, did they contribute to the event or meeting? This can be measured by getting feedback from the audience

by running focus groups with a sample of the audience, or using technical data to monitor websites.

3. *Audience Action.* This involves tracking progress on awareness and development levels and will involve more detailed research with the targeted audience prior to, during and after completion of the campaign activities.

Example

Research commissioned by the Disability Rights Commission (DRC) revealed that young disabled people lacked confidence to use public transport. Forster designed a communications campaign, GOJO, to address the issue among 16- to 25-year-olds in five UK regions. The aim was to increase confidence levels, leading to more journeys by young disabled people on public transport, as well as raising awareness of new rights in discrimination laws.

The main focus of the campaign was a website that provided practical information and details of how to complain to transport operators. It encouraged interaction via a blog where users recorded their travel experiences and offered tips. Forster also undertook stakeholder relations targeting transport providers and those that worked with disabled people.

Evaluation of the website during the 11 weeks of campaign activities showed that 78 per cent of website sessions (21,597) did not come through a referral website, reflecting on the success of online PR. It also showed that the link that achieved the most referrals to the site was from the Direct Gov website. Forster's qualitative and quantitative pre- and post-campaign research found that 70 per cent of respondents said that GOJO had influenced them to use public transport.

These examples illustrate how good sustainable practices utilise the People element of TBL (Figure 11.5) in conjunction with the Planet and Profit elements.

Figure 11.5 Fundamentals for good PR practice

Ultimately the demand for sustainable business practices is here to stay and is going to increase with every passing year. As Kotler says, 'There's no turning back.'

Summary and activities

Key points

- **Buying is always guided by consumers' thoughts, feelings and actions, and since we take on attitudes, beliefs, opinions and values from others, companies that are not aware of changes in society run the risk of alienating customers.**

- All companies are located on the sustainability continuum and need to be aware of their position in order to be able to position (or reposition) themselves within their markets by making effective strategic and operational decisions.
- You will need to look towards operating in an increasingly sustainable fashion. Hence, you may need to benchmark your current performance and identify (and remove) barriers to adopting sustainability
- There are many support mechanisms available to you, including codes of conduct, trade bodies, guides, business standards and business schools, not to mention PR agencies and consultants.

Activities

There's precious little on sustainable marketing even in the key marketing texts. To look at a range of academic conference papers (which cover a large range of industries around the world), go to the Corporate Responsibility Research Conference website (http://www.crrconference.org).

The following book contains a number of informative studies on sustainability, including the key Hart and Elkington studies:

Welford, R and Starkey, R (2001) *The Earthscan Reader in Business and Sustainable Development*, Earthscan, London

Have a look at the Co-operative's CSR platform; it's as good as any in the world. It's transparent and independently audited, and the Co-operative refuses to take business that contradicts its ethical policies. Also look up the FTSE4GOOD index.

Answers to questions

1 Public relations in business: an introduction

1. PR operates at all levels of any organisation, as all employees are ambassadors for your brand. PR can operate tactically, working across all functions of the business, promoting the organisation internally and externally. It can contribute to the boardroom discussions. PR is most effective if it is understood and endorsed by the senior management and if it underpins business objectives. At its best, it permeates every decision the business makes and every strategic aim it has.
2. The Data Protection Act 1998 restricts the amount of information PRs are able to release about individuals who may be being investigated by the press. It also helps PRs protect vulnerable people from public scrutiny. The Freedom of Information Act 2000 means that journalists can ask questions of public-sector organisations, but it gives PRs the time to investigate the requests thoroughly, as you can have up to 20 working days to respond to FOI requests. Privacy laws, including the Human

Rights Act 2000, provide rights to privacy and confidentiality for individuals that protect them from being exposed in the press.

3. PR can be implemented by an individual in an organisation who maybe already does marketing for your business. Courses run by the CIPR and institutions like Leeds Business School can help embed good PR understanding and practices. Consultancies and PR agencies are also available to offer more comprehensive, tailored PR for your business.

2 Where PR sits with advertising and marketing

1. Noise involves understanding and interpreting the plethora of distractions that your messages may face when transmitted through differing media. This ultimately can affect the decoding or customers' interpretation of your message. If the customer can't see the wood for the trees, you'll need to encode your message in a different way.

2. Because we're wired up to continuously communicate in a range of ways: audio, visual, textural, smell, and so on. These stimuli are happening all of the time and the combination of fragmented markets and oversupply means we all have to work at how we communicate with our stakeholder continuously.

3. An opinion leader is someone whom the target market sees as having a social standing and influence generally. An opinion former is such owing to their actual expertise, usually through their profession, which means that they have credibility.

3 Understanding strategic public relations

1. The PEST factors constitute the key forces in the macro-environment: social, technological, economic,

environmental, legal, political, informational, ethical and sustainable.

2. The micro-environment consists of customers, competitors, suppliers, distributors, publics, facilitators, employers, employees, unions, shareholders, financiers, manufacturers, agents, franchises, intermediaries, lawyers, agencies, journalists, investors and plumbers!

3. The micro-environment is partly controllable and influenced because of the relationships that the organisation has with the relevant parties. The influence varies depending on circumstances, for example in a crisis.

4. The monitoring of the environment is very much dependent upon the nature of the industry, market and environment you see yourself operating in. Ideally, you should be monitoring the environment daily, even in a stable climate. The macro-environment is turbulent and dynamic; anything can happen!

4   Working with the media

1. Remember that most news items have a human element angle, even if this involves including a quote from a credible source. Make sure you can address the who, what, where, when, why and how of each news release. If you can answer these questions and your release is newsworthy, then you've the basics of a news release.

2. Journalists are busy people, under huge pressure to meet tight deadlines and engage their audiences. Getting to know your key journalists is a good way to develop a professional relationship with them. Try to create an opportunity to meet them to introduce your organisation and explore how you can help the journalist to deliver great news articles to their target audience.

3. Good photography and graphics are well worth investing in to enhance your news stories. Consider the content of the photograph to enhance the story and create more coverage of your story. Think of the composition; more than three people in a photo can get too busy. Giving a photographer a brief that

is clear but allows for creativity is important. Increasingly, PRs are developing video news releases and audio news releases to sell in their stories to the media.

5 PR and developments in online communications

1. As audiences and technology become more sophisticated, the need to generate two-way communication and interactive websites is increasing. No longer is it relevant to post new pages on your website without creating the opportunity for visitors to the site to respond in some way. This relationship with visitors to your site is more meaningful and more likely to generate repeat visits and collection of data regarding visitors to your site which you can use for future communication and relationship development.

2. Online coverage lasts longer than printed coverage because it is still available days, months and often years after first appearing. The opportunity to develop links to other websites and generate RSS feeds adds to the Long Tail effect, identified by Chris Anderson. This is great if all your coverage is positive, but not so good if there is some negative coverage. To overcome this you must keep posting new positive articles on your social media sites and websites.

6 Stakeholders and customers: how to develop and maximise relations

1. When consumers are making a risky decision, whether it be financially risky or personally or socially risky (or all these!), they tend to take their time making the decision, searching for information and weighing up the pros and cons.

2. Factors such as sex, age, occupation, income, their personality type, sense of motivation and perception, and past experiences will all serve to influence consumers' choices and behaviour.
3. Businesses purchase in significantly larger volumes than consumers. They also have a degree of specialised purchasing skill which the average consumer does not tend to have. The procedures and policies of purchasing by a business also tend to be more formal and often include several people.

7 Crisis, what crisis?

1. During a crisis the key element is to ensure that the organisation maintains an element of control of the situation. It can do this by establishing a crisis management team early on. Proactively looking for sensitive ways to overcome negative media and public reaction can reduce the impact, as can keeping in touch with the media on a proactive and reactive basis.
2. Good relations with the media during calmer times can be very useful during a crisis. Issuing statements rather than putting a person up for interview will help you to control the messages and reduce the need for journalists to come onto your premises looking for answers.
3. Staff should be fully trained in the role they will play during a crisis, and the importance of not speaking to the press. All media enquiries should be handled by a dedicated team or an individual who has seniority and experience of dealing with the media.

8 Internal communications

1. Companies that engage in internal communications recognise the benefits of having an enthusiastic workforce. Effective internal communications can increase productivity and profitability. It can reduce sickness rates, absenteeism and

staff turnover. As Rosabeth Moss Kanter says, 'Leaders must wake people out of inertia.'

2. Organisations that have good internal communications usually have good external communications or PR, but the same is not always true in reverse. Internal communications is a growing discipline within public relations, traditionally practised by journalists or the HR function. It is a highly strategic discipline that commands experience and a strong track record of success among employers. It is one of the areas of growth within marcomms as employers strive to reduce employment costs and increase productivity.

3. A range of tools is available to internal communications specialists. As a strategic discipline, internal communications requires research, via for example audits, including focus groups and questionnaires, to ensure that employees are able to engage effectively with a range of means of communication such as weekly newsletters, video and audio messages, events and intranets and to maintain overall satisfaction. On a local level it encourages discussion among department teams, with the opportunity to feedback good and bad practice within the organisation without fear of reprisal, and acknowledgement of the value of the contributions being made by staff.

9   Getting the facts right: using research to create a competitive edge

1. Investment in marketing research is crucial to provide accurate data to help make more informed decisions, lower risk and generate greater knowledge. Secondary data are data that already exist in some shape or form. The use of past sales or market research reports, articles and government statistics are all examples. Primary data are data that are collected first-hand to help solve the actual research problem and fulfil the research objectives. The use and creation of a questionnaire, in-depth

interviews, focus groups, observation and experimentation are all examples of how primary data can be collected.

2. Research can be time-consuming and costly, both financially and through the use of additional resources. A degree of expertise is also required at times.

3. Research objectives serve to provide focus, a sense of purpose and direction to the research. They tend to govern the choice of secondary and primary data and the overall design of the research itself.

References

Elkington, J (1998) The 'triple bottom line' for 21st century business, published in R Welford and R Starkey (eds) (2001) *The Earthscan Reader in Business and Sustainable Development*, Earthscan, London

Grewal, D and Salovey, P (2005) Feeling smart: the science of emotional intelligence, *American Scientist*, **93**, pp 330–39

Hart, N A (ed) (1996) *The CIM Marketing Dictionary*, 5th edn, Butterworth-Heinemann, Oxford

Hart, S L (1997) Beyond greening: strategies for a sustainable world, published in R Welford and R Starkey (eds) (2001) *The Earthscan Reader in Business and Sustainable Development*, Earthscan, London

Howell, R [accessed 20 February 2008] Global trade and sustainable development: complementary or contradictory?, paper for Corporate Responsibility Research Conference, Dublin, July 2006 [Online] http://crrconference.org

Imber, J and Toffler, B (2008) *Dictionary of Marketing Terms*, 4th edn, Barron's Educational Series, New York

Ivanovic, A and Collin, P H (2003) *Dictionary of Marketing: Over 7,000 terms clearly defined*, Bloomsbury, London

Kotler, P, Wong, V, Saunders, J and Armstrong, G (2005) *Principles of Marketing*, 4th European edn, Prentice Hall, Harlow

McGoldrick, P (2002) *Retail Marketing*, 2nd edn, McGraw-Hill, Maidenhead

Raj, R and Musgrave, J (2009) *Event Management and Sustainability*, CABI, Wallingford

Richardson, N (2008) To what extent have key retail and generic marketing texts adopted sustainability?, *World Journal of Retail Business Management*, **2** (4), 47–55

Shannon, C E and Weaver, W (1963) *The Mathematical Theory of Communication*, University of Illinois Press, Urbana